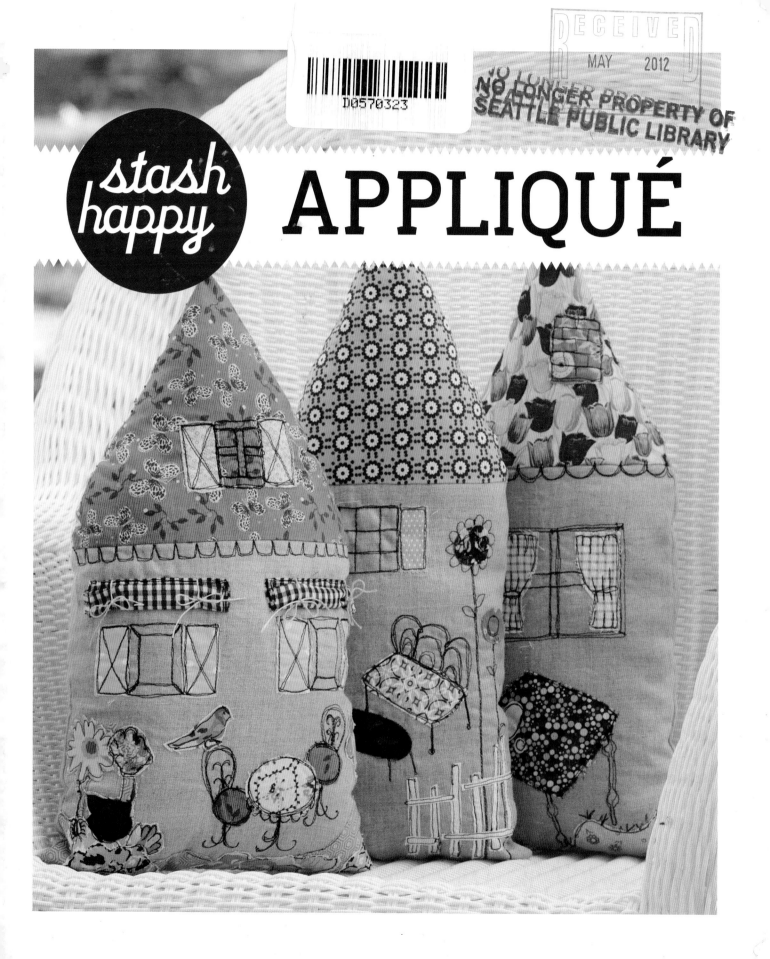

stash happy
APPLIQUÉ

stash happy

APPLIQUÉ

25 FRESH PROJECTS FOR FABRIC LOVERS

Cynthia Shaffer

LARK CRAFTS
Asheville

EDITOR: *Thom O'Hearn*

WRITER & EDITOR: *Jenny Doh*

COPY EDITOR: *Rebecca Behan*

ASSISTANT EDITORS: *Nancy D. Wood,*
Jana Holstein

ART DIRECTOR: *Megan Kirby*

DESIGNER: *Raquel Joya*

PHOTOGRAPHER: *Cynthia Shaffer*

COVER DESIGNER: *Pamela Norman*

LARK CRAFTS

An Imprint of Sterling Publishing
387 Park Avenue South
New York, NY 10016

If you have questions or comments about this book, please visit: larkcrafts.com

Library of Congress Cataloging-in-Publication Data

Shaffer, Cynthia.
  Stash happy : appliqué : 30 fresh projects for fabric lovers / Cynthia Shaffer. -- 1st ed.
      p. cm.
  Includes index.
  ISBN 978-1-4547-0280-1
  1. Appliqué --Patterns. I. Title. II. Title: Appliqué : 30 fresh projects for fabric lovers.
  TT779.S44 2012
  746.44'5--dc23
                                    2011031993
10 9 8 7 6 5 4 3 2 1

First Edition

Published by Lark Crafts
An Imprint of Sterling Publishing Co., Inc.
387 Park Avenue South, New York, NY 10016

Distributed in Canada by Sterling Publishing,
c/o Canadian Manda Group, 165 Dufferin Street
Toronto, Ontario, Canada M6K 3H6

Distributed in the United Kingdom by GMC Distribution Services,
Castle Place, 166 High Street, Lewes, East Sussex, England BN7 1XU

Distributed in Australia by Capricorn Link (Australia) Pty Ltd.,
P.O. Box 704, Windsor, NSW 2756 Australia

Manufactured in China

ISBN 13: 978-1-4547-0280-1

For information about custom editions, special sales, and premium and corporate purchases,
please contact Sterling Special Sales Department at 800-805-5489 or specialsales@sterlingpub.com.

For information about desk and examination copies available to college and university
professors, requests must be submitted to academic@larkbooks.com. Our complete policy
can be found at www.larkcrafts.com.

page 26

page 110

page 90

page 74

stash happy APPLIQUÉ

online!

Find a handful of free bonus
projects at
www.larkcrafts.com/bonus.

It's the perfect day to appliqué!

Appliqué is nothing short of magic. With a pinch of fabric and a few stitches, you can create objects to inspire, bring joy, and make anyone feel special! It's a craft where no fabric scrap gets left behind, as even the smallest bit or bob can be incorporated into handmade wonders that beautify your home, your office, or your wardrobe.

Fabulous fat quarters? Charming charm packs? Leftovers from Stash Happy: Felt? *Whatever you have onhand is probably perfect for appliqué! Patterns and colors you love can transform even the most basic store-bought items into ones that are just right for you.*

You will discover that there are many different ways to appliqué. Some of the methods you will learn include frayed raw edge, turned edge, needle turn, satin stitch, open zigzag, trapunto, and reverse appliqué.

For those of you who are frequently on-the-go, you'll discover that appliqué is positively portable, especially projects that mainly use stash fabrics. Whether you're on the couch watching your favorite show, in the car headed to visit the in-laws, or at the ballpark cheering as your kid slides into home plate, there's hardly any activity that doesn't pair well with a bit of appliqué-to-go.

As you flip through these projects, you'll get a glimpse into my personal stash. But when you reach for fabric pieces from your own beloved pile of fabrics, the projects will become uniquely and undeniably your very own!

- *Let the littlest ones in your life know you care with a very special appliquéd set for baby (page 52) or an adorable tooth fairy pillow (page 64) for your young child.*

- *Update your favorite living room by adding splashes of color to an ordinary lampshade (page 30) and creating a set of house-shaped pillows (page 18) for the couch.*

- *Strut your style with a super cute embellished pair of Mary Jane shoes (page 23), an altered trench with matching covered buttons (page 97), or a distinctively playful appliquéd watch (page 60).*

- *Impress friends and family with truly unique gifts like a soft and cuddly gnome doll (page 70), or birdy apron set (page 100).*

Start right now—today's a great day to get stash happy!

basics

gather

The projects are designed so that you can pull some fabrics from your stash, some items from the Basic Appliqué Sewing Kit, and just go! As you're reaching for your stash, take note of the thoughts I share about the fabrics I favor for appliqué and a few other key materials. Some projects use other items that you have too...

To the Stash...and Beyond!

My go-to fabric for appliqué is quilting cotton. Visit any quilt or fabric store to select from the latest colors and patterns. Precut "fat quarters," widely available at quilt shops and fabric stores, are also great for building your stash. Half a yard of fabric that is cut on the fold yields two fat quarters that each measures 18 x 22 inches (45.7 x 55.9 cm). This fabric

size opens up many options when cutting fabric for appliqué.

In addition to quilting cottons, the projects incorporate these additional fabrics from my stash:

- Drill
- Felt
- Flannel
- Jersey
- Linen
- Muslin
- Osnaberg
- Wool or silk suiting

You will notice that none of the fabrics listed are sheer fabrics. That's because sheer fabrics are usually slippery and hard to manipulate when using appliqué techniques. So consider yourself warned!

basic appliqué sewing kit

* Sewing machine
* Rotary cutter + mat + quilting ruler
* Scissors
* Pinking shears
* Measuring tape + ruler
* Straight pins
* Safety pins
* Fabric spray adhesive
* Iron + pressing cloth
* Water-soluble fabric marker + sharp pencil
* Fray retardant
* Hand-sewing and embroidery needles
* Pointy utensil for turning

beyond THE FABRIC

- *Embroidery floss:* You'll see embroidery floss used throughout this book. Many of the projects use it to attach appliquéd shapes to base fabrics and to add embellishments. For stellar results, I recommend gathering plenty of six-strand cotton embroidery floss in assorted colors.

- *Perle cotton:* If you want your hand embroidery stitches to really pop, consider using perle cotton. The 100 percent mercerized two-ply cotton is heftier and shinier than

embroidery floss and it comes in five different weights. You'll want to equip your stash with plenty of this versatile material.

- *Interfacing:* Some projects require the use of interfacing to strengthen or stabilize the fabric. Fusible interfacing melts and fuses with fabrics when heated with an iron, and it's easy to work with. Non-fusible interfacing does not melt, and therefore must be stitched onto fabric. Different projects require different types of

interfacing and I recommend stocking up on both for your appliqué stash.

- *Forget-Me-Not:* Don't forget about ribbons, buttons, fun trims, binding and bias tape, polyester fiberfill, and assorted threads for machine- and hand-stitches. I consider these notions the part of my stash that can make a project extra special—so be sure to stock up on these goodies!

make
Using Templates

In the back of the book, you'll find all of the templates you need to make the projects. Size the templates based on the percentages listed. Once you have the correct size printed out on paper, cut out the paper template pieces and then follow the individual project instructions for using them. Keep your templates in a clearly marked envelope so you can use them again in the future. There are a few different ways that you can use templates for appliqué.

Paper-Backed Fusible Web:

This material is ideal for raw-edge appliqué. Think of it as a layer of adhesive that melts when it's heated with an iron. All you do is fuse the web onto the wrong side of the fabric, trace the cut templates on the paper side of the fused fabric, and cut out the shapes. Then peel off the paper backing and fuse the appliqué to the base fabric with an iron. Add hand or machine stitches to finish. Keep in mind that for this technique, the right side of the template needs to be placed on the paper side of the fusible web to yield a final appliqué that is properly oriented.

Freezer Paper:

This material is ideal for turned edge appliqué. Freezer paper—found in the grocery store near the aluminum foil—has a shiny, waxy side and a dull paper side. Trace the right sides of the templates onto the dull paper side of the freezer paper using a pencil, and cut it out. Iron the waxy side of each cut template onto the wrong side of the fabric. Then cut out the fabric, adding about ¼ inch (6 mm) around the entire template shape. Fold this seam allowance over the freezer paper side of the piece and use scissors to clip any convex curves and notch any concave curves. Press the seam allowance under all the way around each piece. Remove the freezer paper and appliqué each piece onto base fabric.

Templar:

This material is a heat-resistant plastic available at quilt shops, and is also ideal for needle-turn appliqué. Trace each template shape onto the templar using a fine-point permanent marker and cut it out. Then, using a washable fabric marker, trace the templates onto the wrong side of the fabric, and cut the fabric, adding about ¼ inch (6 mm) around the entire template shape. Place the templar templates back onto the fabric, apply liquid starch around the template edges with a small paintbrush, and iron the edges onto the template. Let cool, remove the template, and then press the edges of the appliqué once more. Either hand-baste or use spray adhesive to place the appliquéd shape onto the base fabric, and then stitch it in place.

Cut It Out!

Cutting fabric for appliqué is straightforward. When cutting specific measurements, use a rotary system to create nice, neat squares and strips. When cutting with a template, all you need is a pair of sharp scissors and a steady hand.

Some projects will ask you to cut out part of a special patterned fabric to highlight a special motif. This process is called "fussy" cutting, which simply means to cut around the pattern in the fabric so the motif is featured in the appliqué.

Oh the Ways You'll Appliqué

Now that everything has been prepped and cut, it's time to select an appliqué method. Remember that just because a project uses one method doesn't mean you can't mix things up. Feel free to interchange, substitute, and alter the methods to suit your preferences. Machine appliqué does not require any special foot for the sewing machine. However, having a walking foot would be helpful when you are quilting layers of fabric and batting, especially for projects like the Mug Rugs (page 14) and Tic-Tac-Toe gameboard (page 47). The walking foot is used for machine quilting and has its own set of upper feed dogs that work in conjunction with the machine's feed dogs to help move layers of fabric through the machine with ease.

Frayed Raw Edge

If you want instant gratification, this is the method for you. You just cut and sew, without worrying about seam allowances or turning under the fabric edges. Paper-backed fusible web makes this process simple because you can attach the cut appliqué directly onto the base fabric with a hot iron. Once the appliqué is in place, you can machine-stitch or hand-sew fairly close to the edges for added fabulousness. With raw-edge appliqué, I like to stitch around the design twice because it secures the stitches and gives the project a nice, sketch-like feel **(fig. A)**.

Turned Edge

This method takes more time than frayed raw-edge appliqué, but if you have the patience, you will enjoy the finished look that the method achieves. Freezer paper and templar are the two main options for working with turned edge appliqué. With either material, you are essentially turning under the edges of the appliqué shape by approximately ¼ inch (6 mm) and stitching it in place. I recommend using the blind stitch to attach the appliqué so that the stitching will not show **(fig. B)**.

Needle Turn

Needle turn is a form of turned-edge appliqué. It is a process that does not involve materials like freezer paper or templar. Rather, you baste the cut appliqué piece onto the base fabric and use the hand-sewing needle to turn under the edges of the appliqué while you stitch. It is convenient because there is hardly any prep work involved; however it is a traditional method that requires lots of practice and patience to do well.

Satin Stitch

For this method, set your sewing machine for a closely spaced zigzag stitch of the desired width. Cut the appliqué to the desired finished size without adding any seam allowance and tack it down to the base fabric. If the appliqué shape is curvy, make sure to raise your machine's presser foot while the needle is down as you ease the appliqué around the curves. Once the stitching is done, trim away raw or loose threads **(fig. C)**.

Open Zigzag

In contrast to the tight satin stitch, the open zigzag is more opened spaced.

fig. A

fig. B

fig. C

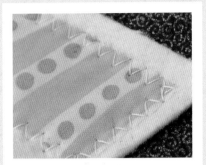

fig. D

fig. E

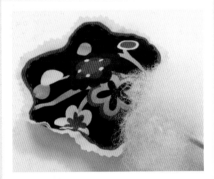

fig. F

fig. G

Simply adjust the zigzag width and length. It's a quick and easy option that pairs well with raw-edge appliqué as it reinforces the edges (**fig. D**).

Blanket Stitch

Also known as the buttonhole stitch, the blanket stitch reinforces either raw-edge or turned-edge appliqué. Refer to the Handy Hand Stitches guide (opposite page) for information on creating the blanket stitch by hand. Many modern sewing machines have a built-in blanket stitch option, if you prefer to machine-stitch (**fig. E**).

Trapunto

This method is known as the "stuffed technique" because it creates a puffy effect. I like to stitch the appliqué motif onto a stiffer backing fabric like cotton or drill. Once it's stitched, slit the backing fabric (or leave a small opening) and stuff with polyester fiberfill. Remember that a little bit of stuffing goes a long way, so don't overdo it! If the backside of the appliqué will be visible, whipstitch the slit closed (**fig. F**).

Reverse Appliqué

For most appliqué methods, the specialty fabric is placed on top of the base fabric and stitched down. For reverse appliqué, the specialty fabric is placed beneath the base fabric, the layers are stitched together, and then the base fabric is cut away to reveal the specialty fabric that peeks through the opening (**fig. G**).

Extra Touches = Extra-Ordinary

With all good appliqué projects, there are extra touches that you can add to get extraordinary results.

Q is for Quilting

Many of the projects involve making a "quilt sandwich," as you would when making a traditional quilt (for example, the Mug Rugs on page 14). The sandwich consists of three layers: the appliquéd top fabric (right side facing up), the batting, and the backing fabric (right side facing down). When you're stitching through these layers, you've got several options as follows.

Stitch in the Ditch: Stitch into the seams created by your patchwork process, so that your stitch lines are almost invisible.

Straight Stitch: Create straight lines of quilting. You can stitch the lines in one direction or mix vertical, horizontal, and diagonal lines for added interest (**fig. H**).

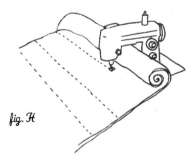

fig. H

Free-motion: Lower the feed dogs on your sewing machine and attach a darning foot, then guide the fabric in any direction to create free-form stitches. A common free-motion quilting method, called stippling, creates a continuous, meandering line of stitches **(fig. I)**.

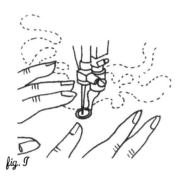

fig. I

Patchwork: Within traditional quilting, patchwork is the process of sewing together pieces of fabric to create a larger design. The Mug Rugs (page 14), Pouch (page 82) and the Tic-Tac-Toe gameboard (page 47) involve patchwork, for example. The key to successful patchwork is to use a cutting mat, rotary cutter, and quilting ruler to precisely measure and cut the fabric pieces as uniformly as possible. Attach the cut pieces using a straight stitch and a ¼-inch (6 mm) seam allowance. Press seam allowances as instructed for each project.

Embroidery and Hand Stitches

I'm sure you can tell by the projects that I'm a big fan of embroidery. No matter the method for appliqué, you can always enhance the design and customize it to your liking by adding hand stitches. This handy chart illustrates all the stitches you'll need to know to make the projects in this book.

HANDY HAND *stitches*

BACKSTITCH

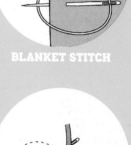

BLANKET STITCH

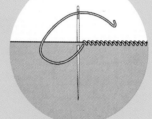

OVERCAST STITCH

FRENCH KNOT

RUNNING STITCH

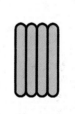

SATIN STITCH

BLIND STITCH

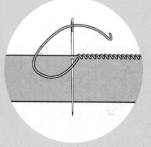

WHIPSTITCH

The Ties that Bind

Sometimes frayed edges are desirable on small, quilted projects; other times, you'll want to add polish by finishing a project with a nicely bound edge. The tic-tac-toe project (page 47) is a great example of using binding to create a nicely finished edge.

Making Your Own Custom Bias Tape

When a project calls for bias tape, you can either use purchased bias tape or create your own. My favorite way of making custom bias tape is to cut strips from a square and stitch them together. Here's how:

❶ Lay a square piece of fabric onto the cutting mat, with the right side facing you.

❷ Draw parallel lines with a pencil and ruler at a 45-degree angle (on the bias), spaced ½ to 2 inches (1.3 to 5.1 cm) apart, as listed in the project instructions.

❸ Pin two of the cut strips, right sides together, to form a right angle with the ¼-inch (6 mm) tips from one strip extending beyond the other strip (**fig. J**). Stitch together using a ¼-inch (.6 mm) seam allowance and snip the tips from either side. Continue stitching additional strips to create the desired length. Press the seam allowances open (**fig. K**).

❹ Press the stitched strip down the center, lengthwise (**fig. L**).

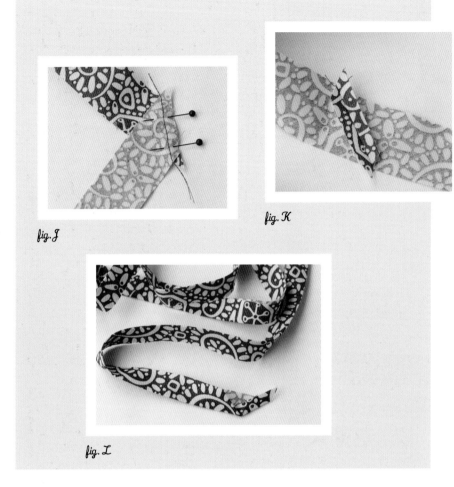

fig. J

fig. K

fig. L

Custom Binding Cut on the Straight of Grain

If cutting on the bias for your binding is not necessary, cutting binding on the straight of grain is a quick and easy alternative.

❶ Measure and calculate the length of the binding needed, plus a little extra to account for the overlap at the start, and for turning the corners.

❷ Lay a square shape of fabric onto the cutting mat, with the right side facing you.

❸ Cut fabric strips on the straight of the grain, pin the short ends of the strips together at a right angle, with right sides facing, and stitch diagonally across the corner (**fig. M**). Trim the seam allowance (**fig. N**) and press the seams open (**fig. O**).

❹ Press the stitched strip down the center, lengthwise (**fig. P**).

Binding with Mitered Corners

❶ Lay your project flat and trim the layers of all edges uniformly. (This is called truing up a project.)

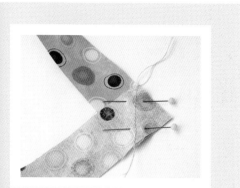

fig. M

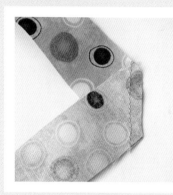

fig. N

fig. O

fig. P

❷ Starting midway on one edge and folding the starting edge to the wrong side, pin and stitch the right side of the binding to the right side of the fabric.

❸ Stop stitching ¼ inch (6 mm) before you reach the first corner, and backstitch **(fig. Q)**.

❹ Take your work off of the machine, and fold the binding straight up over itself to form a 45-degree angle at the corner **(fig. R)**. Fold the binding straight down so that its raw edge is even with the next edge, pin **(fig. S)**, and then stitch. Repeat this process for all the other corners.

❺ When you near the starting point, stitch the binding strip over the starting edge of the binding (where it's already been folded over).

❻ Fold the binding over the edges to the back. Turn under the raw edge enough to cover the seam that you just stitched **(fig. T)**. Place the prepared edge barely over the seam line that attached the binding and pin it down along the edges. Create diagonal folds at the corners and pin **(fig. U)**.

❼ Working from the back, use a blind stitch to attach the binding. Working from the front, stitch in the ditch.

fig. Q

fig. R

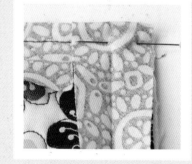

fig. S

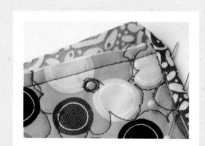

fig. T

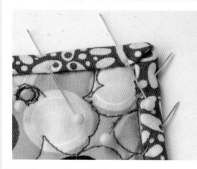

fig. U

scrappy & scrumptious MUG RUGS

The perfect spot to rest your mug, and a cookie, too!

from your stash

¼ yard (.23 m) of felt

¼ yard (.23 m) of neutral fabric like linen, osnaburg, or cotton

Assorted fabric scraps, including cottons, wool suiting, and/or silk

Fabric scrap printed with words or phrases (optional)

gather

Basic appliqué sewing kit (page 7)

Templates (page 121)

¼ yard (.23 m) batting

¼ yard (.23 m) paper-backed fusible web

make

1 Cut assorted fabric scraps into strips that measure 1¼ to 2 inches (3.2 to 5.1 cm) wide and 6½ inches (16.5 cm) in length.

2 Piece the strips together, using a ¼-inch (6-mm) seam allowance, until the unit measures 10 inches (25.4 cm) wide. True up the entire unit, using a rotary cutter, ruler, and cutting mat, to measure 6½ x 10 inches (16.5 x 25.4 cm).

3 Cut a piece of felt and a piece of batting to the same size as the sewn piece. Make a quilt sandwich (page 10) with the felt, batting, and sewn piece.

4 Stitch around the perimeter of the quilt sandwich. Stitch around the perimeter of these layers using a ¼-inch (6-mm) seam allowance **(fig. A)**.

5 Machine-quilt straight lines across the layers, varying the widths between lines from ¼ to ⅜ inch (6 to 9.5 mm). Embrace the wonky and deliberately imperfect feel that these stitch lines provide.

6 Repeat steps steps 1–5 to make the second Mug Rug.

fig. A

fig. B

fig. C

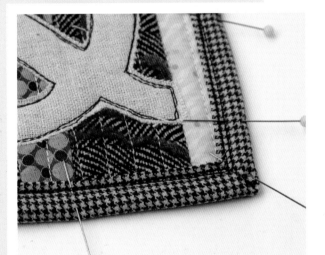

fig. D

fig. E

appliqué

7 Press the paper-backed fusible web onto the back side of the neutral fabric piece.

8 Enlarge and cut out the ampersand and asterisk templates. Trace each onto the neutral fabric, placing the right side of templates onto the paper side of the fused fabric. Cut out the shapes.

9 Peel the paper backing off each appliqué, position on the side of the quilted unit, and press on the appliqués.

10 Topstitch each appliqué with two rows of stitching to secure **(fig. B)**.

bind

11 Create binding (page 12) with the remaining scraps of assorted fabric to make a strip that measures 1¼ x 36 inches (3.2 x 91.4 cm). This scrap-piecing method will allow for a "raggedy" feel that complements the scrappy nature of this quilt **(fig. C)**.

12 Use the binding techniques found in the Basics section (pages 12–13) to bind the Mug Rug. However, stitch the binding to the back and turn it to the front. Allow the raw edge of the binding to be exposed and stitch around the perimeter twice **(fig. D)**.

13 Fussy cut a phrase, if desired, from printed fabric and stitch in place **(fig. E)**.

fresh & shabby
PILLOW HOUSES

Create your own adorable scenes on linen with
raw-edge appliqué and free-motion quilting.

from your stash

⅓ yard (.3 m) of linen

¼ yard (.23 m) each of two
coordinating fabrics

Assorted fabric scraps

gather

Basic appliqué sewing kit (page 7)

Templates (page 117)

⅓ yard (.3 m) of lightweight
fusible interfacing

Polyester fiberfill

Large-eye needle

40 inches (102 cm) of hemp yarn

make

❶ Enlarge and cut out template A, and trace it onto the linen twice for the
main body of the house. Cut out the shapes and mark all notches in the seam
allowance.

❷ Enlarge and cut out template B, trace it onto each coordinating fabric, and
cut out the shapes. Using two fabrics for template B ensures that the back side
of the house has a different roof than the front side.

❸ Using template A, cut out one piece of lightweight interfacing for the front
body portion of the house. Use an iron to fuse the interfacing to the wrong
side of the linen piece.

❹ Match the center notches of the front roof fabric with the center notches
on one linen piece, right sides together, and pin in place. Repeat to pin the
back roof fabric to the remaining linen piece (**fig. A**).

fig. A

fig. B

fig. C

fig. D

appliqué

5 Cut parts and pieces from the fabric scraps to create a desired scene. For the pillow shown at right, cut shapes from several fabrics to create a café scene **(fig. B)**.

6 Adhere all the cut fabric pieces to the linen as desired to create your scene, using spray adhesive. Free-motion stitch close to the edges of the adhered fabric scraps, using dark thread. Free-motion stitch to complete the scene, such as the chair backs and windows, as desired **(fig. C)**.

7 To create café curtains, cut two pieces of fabric that each measure 4 x 5 inches (10.2 x 12.7 cm). Position and stitch the top edge of the curtains. Roll up the curtains and tack at the sides to secure **(fig. D)**.

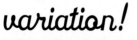

variation!

Change the appliquéd scene to be a castle, barn, fortress, or lighthouse. Don't think too much when you're laying out the scraps.

fig. E

stitch the pillow

❽ Pin together the back and front sides of the house, right sides facing. Double pin at the notches that indicate the start and stopping points **(fig. E)**.

❾ Stitch the pieces together using a ¼-inch (6-mm) seam allowance, pivoting at the corners and rooftop.

❿ Clip the corners at an angle and turn the pillow right side out. Stuff the pillow with polyester fiberfill, fold in the seam allowances, and hand-sew the pillow closed **(fig. F)**.

⓫ Cut the hemp yarn into four 10-inch (25.4 cm) lengths, and thread a large-eye needle with one length. Insert the needle beneath the rolled curtain, bring it up at the top of the curtain, and then tie the yarn tails into a bow. Repeat with the remaining lengths of yarn to secure the other café curtain **(fig. G)**.

fig. F

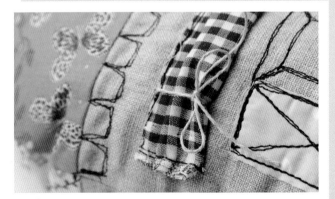

fig. G

modern MARY JANES

Want to add skip to your step? Appliqué these fun shapes onto your favorite pair of fabric shoes.

from your stash

Red fabric scrap with flower (or other) motif

Teal fabric scrap

Muslin scrap (optional)

Perle cotton in red or teal and white

gather

Basic appliqué sewing kit (page 7)

Template (page 120)

Paper-backed fusible web, to fit the fabric scraps

Mary Jane fabric shoes (available at online shoe stores)

Mini iron (available at craft stores, optional)

make

① Iron a piece of paper-backed fusible web onto the wrong sides of the fabric scraps. Cut small circles around the red fabric flower shapes. Copy the template, trace the shape on the fused paper side of the teal fabric, and cut it out **(figs. A–B)**.

② Peel off the paper backing and arrange the motifs as desired on the Mary Jane fabric shoes. Place a contrasting teal-colored fabric motif to add an unexpected color accent.

③ Use the mini iron to fuse each shape in place. If you use a regular size iron, stuff the toe portion of the shoe with muslin so the iron has a firm surface to press against.

④ Stitch a quick overcast stitch around each fabric shape using an embroidery needle and red or teal perle cotton **(fig. C)**.

⑤ Add running stitches around the shapes with teal perle cotton **(fig. D)**.

fig. A

fig. B

fig. C

fig. D

treasures-to-go DRAWSTRING BAG

This clever dish towel-turned-personalized bag can store a collection of toys, craft supplies, or other treasured items.

from your stash

⅛ yard (.1 m) of accent fabric

1 piece of fabric for pocket, 8½ x 10 inches (21.6 x 25.4 cm)

1 piece of fabric for letter, 7 x 7 inches (17.8 x 17.8 cm)

1 piece of fabric for the loop, 8 x 1½ inches (20.3 x 3.8 cm)

Embroidery floss

gather

Basic appliqué sewing kit (page 7)

1 Dish towel, 28 x 18 inches (71.1 x 45.7 cm)

1 piece of batting, 7 x 7 inches (17.8 x 17.8 cm)

Drawstring cording, 50 inches (127 cm)

make

❶ Cut a strip of accent fabric the width of the dish towel. Fussy cut the top edge. Adhere the strip to the dish towel using spray adhesive. Zigzag stitch on the bottom edge, up and around the entire strip of fabric **(fig. A)**.

❷ Turn under the top edge of the pocket flap ½ inch (1.3 cm) to the wrong side and press. Then turn the top pressed edge 1¼ inch (3.2 cm) to the wrong side and stitch at both ends.

❸ Turn the pocket edge right side out. Use a pin or other pointy utensil to push out the corners so they are nice and crisp. Stitch down the folded edge and press the top edge. Press under the bottom and side edges ½ inch (1.3 cm) **(fig. B)**.

fig. A

fig. B

fig. C

appliqué

4 Create a template for the desired letter and cut it out from a coordinating piece of stash fabric. Then cut the shape from the batting with an extra ¼ inch (6 mm) all around the letter.

5 Adhere the fabric letter to the cut batting using spray adhesive. Then adhere the appliqué to the center of the pocket. Zigzag stitch the layers in place **(fig. C)**.

6 Create French knots as desired around the letter, using an embroidery needle and floss.

7 Fold the dish towel in half, wrong sides together. Allowing for the ½-inch (1.3 cm) side seam, center the pocket on the front of the towel. Stitch the sides and bottom edge.

fig. D

fig. E

fig. F

stitch the bag

8 Fold the dish towel in half widthwise, right sides together. Stitch together the sides and bottom, beginning 2 inches (5.1 cm) from the top edge with a backstitch and using a ½-inch (1.3 cm) seam allowance. Turn fabric right side out **(fig. D)**.

9 Turn the top edge 2 inches (5.2 cm) to the outside and topstitch close to the lower edge. This will result in a top casing with a side opening **(fig. E)**.

10 Knot one end of the drawstring cording, stick a safety pin into this end and thread the cording through the casing.

11 Fold under the long edges of the fabric strip for the loop so they meet at the center of the strip. Zigzag stitch to secure. Center and pin the ends to the inside top back of the bag and stitch in place **(fig. F)**.

pretty~ful LAMPSHADE

With a modified trapunto appliqué, this lampshade casts a most unique glow.

from your stash

⅓ yard (.3 m) of large print fabric

⅓ yard (.3 m) of drill or other stable fabric

Perle cotton

gather

Basic appliqué sewing kit (page 7)

Lampshade

Polyester fiberfill

Small beads

make

❶ Fussy cut around the shapes of the large print fabric using pinking shears **(fig. A)**.

❷ Pin the cut pieces on the lampshade, positioning each so that a portion of each piece touches either the top or bottom edge of the lampshade. This will allow the finished appliqué to look grounded **(fig. B)**.

❸ Trace around the pinned shapes using a washable fabric marker and then remove the shapes from the lampshade.

❹ Cut a piece of drill fabric slightly larger than each cut print piece. Pin each print to its corresponding piece of drill fabric and hand-sew together with a running stitch using an embroidery needle and perle cotton. Leave a small opening for stuffing. Trim away the drill close to the running stitch **(fig. C–D)**.

fig. A

fig. B

fig. C

fig. D

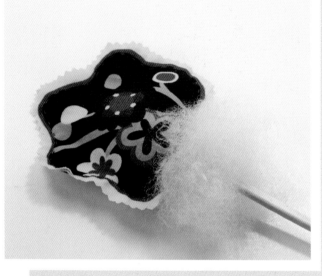

fig. E

fig. F

fig. G

❺ Stuff each appliqué lightly with polyester fiberfil, using a pointy utensil as needed **(fig. E)**, and sew the opening closed. Using spray adhesive, adhere each appliqué to the lampshade as marked in step 3.

❻ Hand-sew the perimeters of the appliquéd shapes to the lampshade with a running stitch Then stitch along the bottom and top edges of the lampshade **(fig. F)**.

❼ Thread the small beads onto perle cotton and sew them on the appliquéd shapes as desired, snugly tying off the thread tails to gently tuft the appliquéd shapes. Erase unwanted fabric pen marks by dabbing them with a damp cloth **(fig. G)**.

time for tea
CAFÉ CURTAINS

Stitch splashes of color onto your plain café curtains with these delectable tea cups.

from your stash
Assorted fabric scraps

gather
Basic appliqué sewing kit (page 7)
Templates (page 127)
Paper-backed fusible web scraps
2 café curtains

make
❶ Trace template A six times onto the paper side of the paper-backed fusible web, flipping over the template to make three tracings in reverse. Trace the saucer (template B), and the tea (template C), six times each onto the paper side of the paper-backed fusible web.

❷ Iron the traced fusible web onto the back sides of three sets of six scrap fabrics and cut out the shapes.

fig. A

fig. B

❸ Peel off the paper backing from the saucer pieces and fuse them onto the curtains as desired using an iron. Peel off the paper backing from the cup pieces and fuse them onto the curtains, partially layered on top of the saucers. Peel off the paper backing from the tea pieces and fuse them onto the top portions of the cups **(fig. A)**.

❹ Stitch all pieces in place using two rows of stitching close to the cut edges of each appliqué **(fig. B)**.

TIP

After you iron the fusible web onto the back side of the fabric (but before you cut out the traced shape), lift up the paper backing and then let it fall back down. This slight lift will help you peel off the paper backing when it is time to remove it.

flower power PENDANTS

Never underestimate the strength
of a cute little fabric pendant.

from your stash

2 pieces of cotton fabric, each 1¾ x 2 inches (4.4 x 5.1 cm)

Fabric scrap

Perle cotton

gather

Basic appliqué sewing kit (page 7)

Template (page 120)

1 piece of batting, 1¾ x 2 inches (4.4 x 5.1 cm)

Batting scrap

Small beads

Craft knife

Jump ring, sized to fit the ball chain

Ball chain

Fray retardant

make

① Layer the piece of batting between the two pieces of cotton fabric with wrong sides together. Adhere these layers using spray adhesive and machine-stitch around the perimeter **(fig A)**.

TIP
To create the lime green pendant, cut the base fabric slightly narrower.

fig. A

fig. B

② Cut out the template and trace it onto the fabric and batting scraps. Cut out the flower shapes and adhere them using fabric spray adhesive.

③ Overcast stitch the flower onto the stitched square, using an embroidery needle and contrasting perle cotton **(fig. B)**.

④ Create a small hole at the top of the square using the craft knife. Reinforce the hole using the embroidery needle and perle cotton, stitching in and out so that the stitches appear to form a small grommet **(fig. C)**.

⑤ Insert the jump ring through the hole and attach the ball chain. Apply fray retardant to the edges of the pendant to prevent fraying. Thread small beads onto perle cotton and stitch them to the center of the flower. Add French knots between the beads.

fig. C

little miss
MASON JARS

Elevate the way sewing notions are stored with these clever cozies designed for the classic mason jar.

from your stash

1 piece of main cotton fabric, 12 x 3¾ inches (30.5 x 9.5 cm)

1 piece of muslin, 12 x 3¾ inches (30.5 x 9.5 cm)

Assorted fabric scraps

Perle cotton

gather

Basic appliqué sewing kit (page 7)

Template (page 120)

1 piece of batting, 12 x 3¾ inches (30.5 x 9.5 cm), plus scraps

Pieced binding, 1¼ x 30 inches (3.2 x 76.2 cm)

3 pieces of elastic, ¼ inch (6 mm) wide, each 2 inches (5.1 cm) long

3 buttons

make

❶ Make a quilt sandwich with the muslin, piece of batting, and main cotton fabric using spray adhesive to adhere the layers together. Stitch around the perimeter using a ¼-inch (6 mm) seam allowance. Choose the desired appliqué design for your jar and complete the appropriate steps that follow.

❷ *Triple button appliqué:* Cut three circles from the fabric scraps and three circles from the batting scraps, each with a diameter of 1¾ inches (4.4 cm). Adhere each fabric circle to a batting circle using spray adhesive, and then adhere the circles as desired to the quilt top. Stitch the perimeters of the circles with a backstitch using an embroidery needle and contrasting perle cotton **(fig. A)**. Create two French knots for "buttonholes" and one straight stitch to connect the two knots **(fig. B)**.

❸ *Spool appliqué:* Cut out the template and trace it onto a fabric scrap and batting scrap. Cut out the shapes and adhere in the same manner as the button appliqué. Backstitch the appliqué onto the quilt top using an embroidery needle and perle cotton.

fig. A

fig. B

fig. C

fig. D

fig. E

❹ *Rickrack appliqué:* Cut a square from a fabric scrap and batting scrap, each 2 inches (5.1 cm) square. Adhere the batting to the back of the fabric, using fabric spray adhesive. Zigzag stitch rows to look like rickrack on the square. Adhere the appliqué square to the quilt top and backstitch around the perimeter.

quilt and bind

❺ After the selected motif is appliquéd to the quilt top, quilt vertical lines ¼ inch (6 mm) apart **(fig. C)**. Stop and start the quilted lines close to the appliquéd motif. Bind the quilted cozy with the prepared binding (pages 12–13).

❻ Fold the elastic pieces in half and pin them, evenly spaced, to the edge of the muslin at one end of the cozy. Stitch in place **(fig. D)**. Attach three buttons, appropriately spaced, to the quilt top at the opposite end of the cozy **(fig. E)**.

pretty little
PAISLEY BROOCH

Paisley can be just the thing to breathe fun into your jacket, sweater, or blouse.

from your stash

Assorted wool felt fabric scraps

Perle cotton

gather

Basic appliqué sewing kit (page 7)

Templates (page 120)

Paper-backed fusible web scraps

Small beads

Pin back

make

1 Cut out and trace templates A, B, and C onto the paper side of the paper-backed fusible web. Flip over template A and trace it onto the back side of a felt scrap.

2 Press the traced fusible web onto the wrong sides of assorted felt scraps and cut out the shapes **(fig. A)**.

3 Peel off the paper backing from the fused A piece and fuse it to the other A piece, wrong sides together.

4 Stitch an overcast stitch around the paisley shape using an embroidery needle and perle cotton.

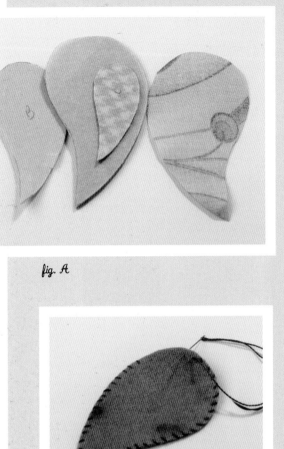

fig. A

fig. B

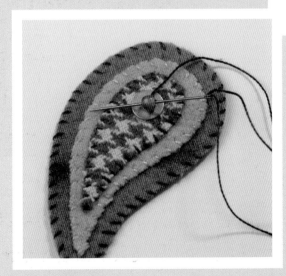

fig. C

5 Peel off the paper backing from the B and C pieces, stack them on top of the fused A piece, and fuse them together using an iron.

6 Hand-sew an overcast stitch around the B and C shapes with coordinating perle cotton. Stitch on small beads as desired at the center of the paisley **(fig. B-C)**.

7 Stitch a pin back to the back side of the brooch **(fig. D)**.

variation!

Create this brooch in two additional sizes by increasing or decreasing the size of the templates. Wear all three on a coat with a larger lapel.

fig. D

colorful & portable TIC-TAC-TOE

A soft gameboard and game pieces can be enjoyed in the comfort of your home or packed up to go in the car, on a plane, or to the park!

from your stash

GAMEBOARD

5 pieces of colored fabric, 3¾ x 3¾ inches (9.5 x 9.5 cm)

4 pieces of white fabric, 3¾ x 3¾ inches (9.5 x 9.5 cm)

2 pieces of border fabric, 1½ x 10¼ inches (3.8 x 25.4 cm)

2 pieces of border fabric, 1½ x 12¼ inches (3.8 x 31.1 cm)

1 piece of backing fabric, 13½ x 13½ inches (34.3 x 34.3 cm)

1 piece of pocket fabric 6¼ x 8½ inches (15.9 x 21.6 cm)

Binding, 2¼ x 55 inches (5.7 x 139.7 cm)

GAME PIECES

¼ yard (.23 m) of green fabric

15 pieces of yellow fabric, 2⅝ x 2⅝ inches (6.7 x 6.7 cm)

Red fabric scrap

Dark-colored perle cotton

gather

Basic appliqué sewing kit (page 7)

Templates (page 116)

1 piece of batting, 13½ x 13½ inches (34.3 x 34.3 cm)

2 buttons

2 pieces of string, 14 inches (35.6 cm) long

10 squares of batting, 2⅝ x 2⅝ inches (6.68 x 6.68 cm)

fig. A

fig. B

fig. C

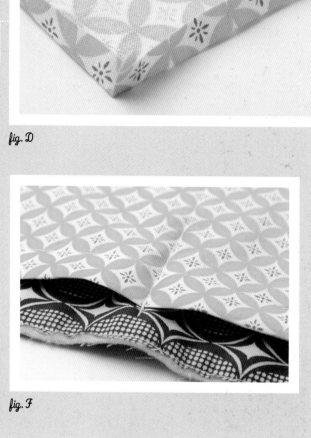

fig. D

fig. E

fig. F

make

gameboard

❶ Arrange the squares of colored and white fabric pieces into three rows of three pieces each, creating a checkerboard motif. Stitch together each row with a ¼-inch (6 mm) seam allowance. Press the seam allowances toward the colored fabric pieces **(fig. A)**.

❷ Stitch the top row to the middle row and the middle row to the bottom row with a ¼-inch (6 mm) seam allowance. Press the seam allowances in the directions they naturally fall.

❸ Stitch the shorter border fabric pieces to the top and bottom of the checkerboard motif and stitch the longer border fabric pieces to the sides of the motif **(fig. B)**.

❹ Make a quilt sandwich (page 10) with the backing fabric, square piece of bating, and the checkerboard motif. Machine-quilt all layers together by stitching in the ditch

(page 10) and by quilting straight vertical and horizontal lines that bisect the checkerboard squares.

❺ Make a double-fold hem on one long edge of the pocket fabric by turning it under ½ inch (1.3 cm), then another 1 inch (2.5 cm). Stitch in place. Turn under the side and bottom edges to the wrong side by ¼-inch (6 mm) **(fig. C–D)**.

❻ Stitch the pocket in place on the back side of the quilted gameboard (shown folded in half in **fig. E**), centered from side to side and 1 inch (2.5 cm) from the edge (which now becomes the top edge).

❼ Attach two buttons toward the bottom of the pocket. Do not sew through to the board. Sew down the middle of the pocket to divide it into a double pocket **(fig. F)**.

fig. I

fig. J

8 Use the binding technique found in the Basics section (page 12–13) to bind the gameboard quilt **(figs. I–J)**.

9 Add a decorative running stitch to the inside of the gameboard using dark perle cotton **(fig. K)**.

10 Tack down the two pieces of string close to the binding, each positioned 4 inches (10.2 cm) from the side edges. Then tack piece again, approximately 2 inches (5.1 cm) from the first tack.

fig. K

fig. L

fig. M

fig. N

game pieces

⑪ Cut out template A and trace it onto the green fabric five times to create the "X" pieces. Cut out template C and trace it onto the green fabric 10 times to create the "O" pieces and onto the batting squares to create five circle-shaped pieces of batting. Cut out the shapes.

⑫ Cut out template B and trace it onto the red fabric scrap to create five heart-shaped pieces **(fig. L)**.

⑬ With fabric spray adhesive, adhere the "X" pieces to five yellow fabric pieces and the heart pieces to five green "O" pieces. Satin stitch in place **(fig. M)**.

⑭ Make five quilt sandwiches with the remaining green fabric circles, the circle-shaped batting pieces, and the appliquéd circles. Use fabric spray adhesive to stick them together.

⑮ Make five quilt sandwiches with the remaining five yellow fabric squares, squares of batting, and the appliquéd square pieces, using spray adhesive.

⑯ Satin stitch the edges of all circle and square layers **(fig. N)**.

⑰ Add a decorative running stitch around each appliqué using perle cotton **(fig. N)**.

sail away
BABY ENSEMBLE

With just a few affordable items from the baby aisle, you can create an ensemble that looks boutique-adorable.

from your stash

Assorted fabric scraps in coordinating colors

1 fat quarter of binding fabric, 18 x 22 inches (45.7 x 55.9 cm)

gather

Basic appliqué sewing kit (page 7)

Templates (page 123)

¼ yard (.23 m) of paper-backed fusible web

2 cloth diapers

Single-fold binding tape

1 jumper

Single-folded binding tape, 25 inches (63.5 cm)

make

bib

1 Cut the paper-backed fusible web to fit and press onto the wrong sides of the assorted fabric scraps.

2 Cut out templates A, B, and C and trace each onto the fabric scraps, right sides facing the paper fusible web. Cut out the shapes. Cut an extra piece from the fused fabric to measure ⅜ x 3½ inches (9.5 mm x 8.9 cm).

3 Cut out template D, pin it onto a cloth diaper, and cut it out to make the bib shape.

4 Arrange the fabric pieces A, B, C, and the fused fabric strip as desired onto bib cutout. Peel off the paper backings and press onto the bib.

5 Secure the appliqués onto the bib using a machine blanket stitch.

fig. A

fig. B

⑥ Bind the outer edge of the bib with the single fold bias tape, following the binding technique found in the Basics section (pages 12–13). Start by stitching the binding to the back side of the bib, then turn and stitch it to the front.

⑦ For the top-edge binding, cut the binding fabric diagonally (on the bias) into two 1¼-inch (3.2-cm) strips. Stitch them together end-to-end to make a strip that is 34 inches (86.4 cm) long. Fold lengthwise and press to make binding (page 12).

⑧ Find the center of the binding strip and pin it to the center front neck edge of the bib. Stitch the binding on the back side, from the midpoint to one end and then from the same midpoint to the other end. Fold over the binding to the front edge, turn under ¼ inch (6 mm), and then topstitch the full length of the binding from end to end to make the neck ties **(fig. A-B)**.

fig. C

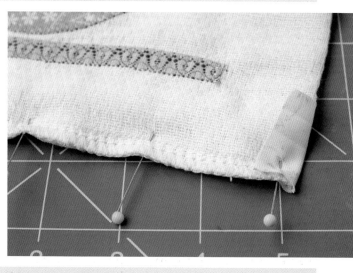

fig. D

jumper

9 Cut out templates E and F and trace each onto leftover prepared fabric scraps, right sides facing the paper side of the fusible web. Cut out the shapes. Cut an exra piece from the fused fabric to measure ⅜ x 3½ inches (9.5 mm x 8.9 cm).

10 Arrange and appliqué the sailboat motif onto the front side of the jumper, following bib instructions, steps 2–5 **(fig. C)**.

burp cloth

11 Cut out templates G, H, and I and trace each onto the remaining leftover prepared fabric scraps once, right sides facing the paper side of the fusible web. Cut out the shapes. Cut an extra piece from the fused fabric to measure ⅜ x 3½ inches (9.5 x 8.9 cm).

12 Arrange and appliqué the sailboat motif onto the front side of the remaining cloth diaper, following bib instructions, steps 2–5.

13 If desired, bind the edges of the burp cloth (page 12–13), measuring the length of bias cut binding needed to fit **(fig. D)**.

dream big!
BANNER

Whip up a decoration that's easy to hang (and change)!

from your stash

⅓ yard (.3 m) of cream felt

Assorted fabric scraps in 5 or 6 coordinating colors

Perle cotton

gather

Basic appliqué sewing kit (page 7)

Templates (page 118)

½ yard (.5 m) of paper-backed fusible web

9 pieces of string or yarn, each 3 inches (7.6 cm) long

Polyester fiberfill

9 buttons

1 piece of ribbon, 1 x 45 inches (2.5 x 114.3 cm)

1 piece of ribbon, 1 x 36 inches (2.5 x 91.4 cm)

1 piece of ribbon, 1 x 20 inches (2.5 x 50.8 cm)

make

① Cut out 9 pairs of rectangles from the felt with pinking shears, 1 pair for each letter as follows:
D—4½ x 6½ inches (11.4 x 16.5 cm)
R—4¼ x 6 inches (10.8 x 15.2 cm)
E—4¾ x 5½ inches (12 x 14 cm)
A—4½ x 6 inches (11.4 x 15.2 cm)
M—5 x 5½ inches (12.7 x 14 cm)
B—4½ x 6½ inches (11.4 x 16.5 cm)
I—3¼ x 6 ½ inches (8.3 x 16.5 cm)
G—4¾ x 6¼ inches (12 x 15.9 cm)
!—3¼ x 6½ inches (8.3 x 16.5 cm)

② Cut the paper-backed fusible web to fit and press onto the wrong sides of the assorted fabric scraps.

③ Cut out the templates and trace each onto the assorted fabric scraps, with the right sides facing the paper-backed fusible web. Cut out the shapes **(fig. A)**.

④ Peel the paper backing off the appliqués, position each on the front panel of the appropriate rectangle pair, and iron on the appliqués.

⑤ Secure the appliquéd pieces onto the felt with red perle cotton using a blanket stitch **(fig. B)**.

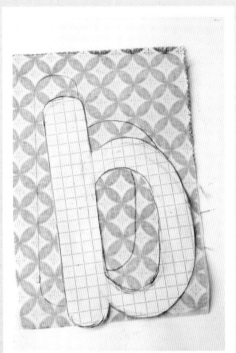

fig. A

fig. B

fig. C

fig. D

assemble

6 Loop the pieces of string and stitch one to the wrong side of each back panel rectangle **(fig. C)**.

7 Hand-sew together the front and back panels for each letter with a running stitch, using red perle cotton, leaving approximately 1 inch (2.5 cm) open at one side for stuffing.

8 Stuff with polyester fiberfill, using a pointy utensil if needed, and then sew each panel closed with a running stitch **(fig. D)**.

finish

9 Stitch a button about 9 inches (22.9 cm) from the top of the 45-inch (114.3 cm) ribbon. Stitch four more buttons to this ribbon, as desired, so that the loops of the stitched panels can be hung on the buttons to create the D-R-E-A-M banner.

10 Stitch three buttons on the 45-inch (114.3 cm) ribbon to hang the B-I-G ! banner, as instructed in step 9.

11 Fold and stitch the top ends of each ribbon in half lengthwise for about 4½ inches (1.4 cm). Fold each stitched section in half and stitch across, forming a loop to hang each banner.

no time like the present
PLAY WATCH

With this watch on, you might not get there on time but you'll get there in style!

from your stash

Assorted fabric scraps in coordinating colors

Perle cotton in black and assorted colors

gather

Basic appliqué sewing kit (page 7)

Templates (page 120)

1 piece of nonwoven medium-weight interfacing, 7 x 5 inches (17.8 x 12.7 cm)

1 scrap of transparency sheet

Permanent black marker

Sewing elastic, ¼ inch (6 mm) wide

1 button

make

watch face

❶ Cut out templates A, B, and C and pin each onto the interfacing. Cut out the shapes. Pin templates A and B onto fabric scraps and cut out. Pin and cut out template C twice.

❷ Layer the piece C interfacing between the fabric C pieces. Adhere these layers using spray adhesive, and blanket stitch around the perimeter using an embroidery needle and perle cotton **(fig. A)**.

❸ Adhere and blanket stitch together the interfacing B piece and the fabric B piece using fabric spray adhesive and perle cotton. Then adhere and stitch this B piece to the large oval made in step 2 **(fig. B)**.

❹ Adhere and stitch together the interfacing A piece and the fabric A piece to make the watch face, using spray adhesive and perle cotton. Embroider the numbers to the watch face with black thread. Add additional embroidery with assorted colors of perle cotton as desired. Embroider the watch hands with black perle cotton **(fig. C)**.

fig. A

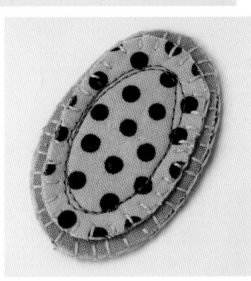

fig. B

fig. C

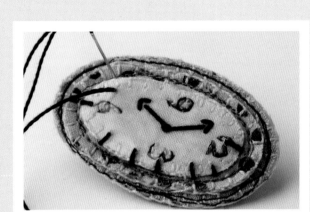

fig. D

fig. E

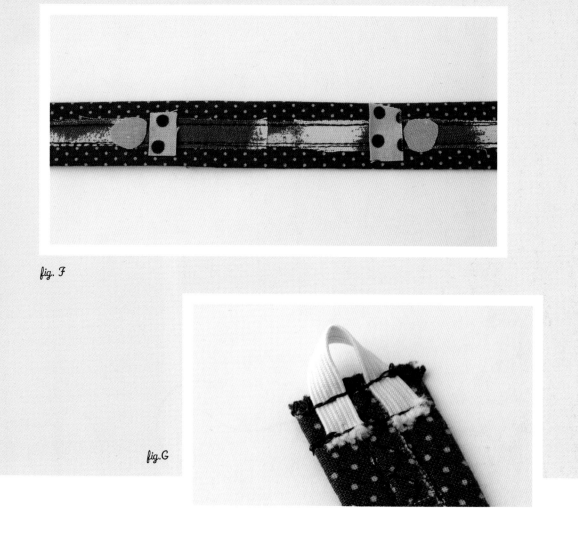

fig. F

fig. G

⑤ Trace template A onto the transparency sheet using a permanent black marker, and cut out the shape.

⑥ Layer and hand-sew together the oval transparency, the watch face, and the stitched medium/large ovals, using each stitch to mark the hours on the clock face **(fig. D)**.

⑦ Cut 2 pieces of elastic that each measure 1⅜ inches (3.5 cm). Pin and stitch each piece to the back side of the watch, using bobbin thread in the same color as the top thread used in

step 6 and making sure the stitches land in the same stitching line **(fig. E)**.

watch band

⑧ Cut the remaining nonwoven medium-weight interfacing to measure ⅞ x 7 inches (2.2 cm x 17.8 cm). Cut a fabric scrap to measure 2¼ x 7 inches (5.7 x 17.8 cm).

⑨ Adhere the interfacing to the center of the cut fabric using spray adhesive. Fold the sides of the fabric over the interfacing and press in place. Zigzag stitch down the center and at both ends of the fabric.

⑩ Cut small circles and strips from fabric scraps and adhere them to the top side of the watch band using spray adhesive. Stitch in place **(fig. F)**.

⑪ Cut a piece of elastic to 2½ inches (6.4 cm). Create a loop and stitch it to one end of the watch band. Attach the button at the other end **(fig. G)**.

⑫ Slide the watchband under the elastic on the watch face, button to close, and enjoy!

sweet dreams
TOOTH PILLOW

With a presentation this special, the tooth fairy will certainly take notice!

from your stash

¼ yard (.23 m) of white fabric

¼ yard (.23 m) of batting

White perle cotton

Metallic embroidery floss

gather

Basic appliqué sewing kit (page 7)

Templates (page 116)

Freezer paper

Spray starch and small bowl (optional)

Small paintbrush (optional)

Pillowcase

Craft knife

make

❶ Cut out template A and trace it onto the dull side of a piece of freezer paper. Cut out the shape, place the shiny side of the paper cutout onto the wrong side of the white fabric, and press. Trim the fabric shape with an added ¼-inch (6 mm) seam allowance. Using template A, cut out the shape from the batting without adding a seam allowance.

❷ Set the batting aside. Clip all curves at the root of the fabric tooth and press the seam allowance toward the centers using the freezer paper as a guide. Spritz spray starch into a small bowl, and use a small brush to apply the starch to the seam allowance to aid in the pressing process **(fig. A)**.

❸ Remove the freezer paper from the clipped and pressed fabric tooth. Place the fabric scraps on top of the corresponding batting piece. Tuck the batting beneath the seam allowance and baste to secure **(fig. B)**.

❹ Repeat steps 1–3 using template A to create a second tooth of the same size.

❺ Cut out template B and follow steps 1–2, to prepare a tooth that is slightly larger than the A-sized teeth. Remove the freezer paper from the clipped and pressed fabric B tooth and place it on top of the batting, but do not baste the layers yet. Set aside.

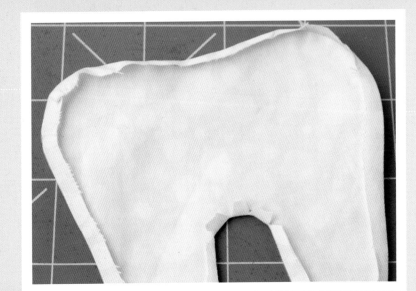

fig. A

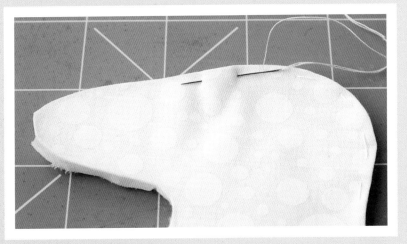

fig. B

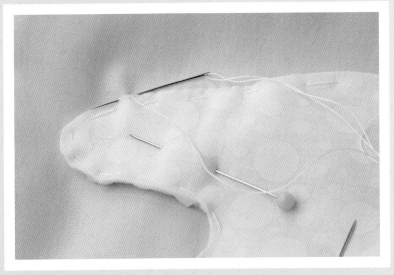

fig. C

appliqué

6 Position the two small teeth onto the pillowcase as shown in the project photo and blind stitch in place **(fig. C)**.

7 Hand quilt along the inside edge of each tooth using an embroidery needle and perle cotton. Echo quilt two rows of running stitch along the outside edges of the teeth.

8 Cut out template C, pin or trace it onto the white fabric, and cut out the shape without adding a seam allowance.

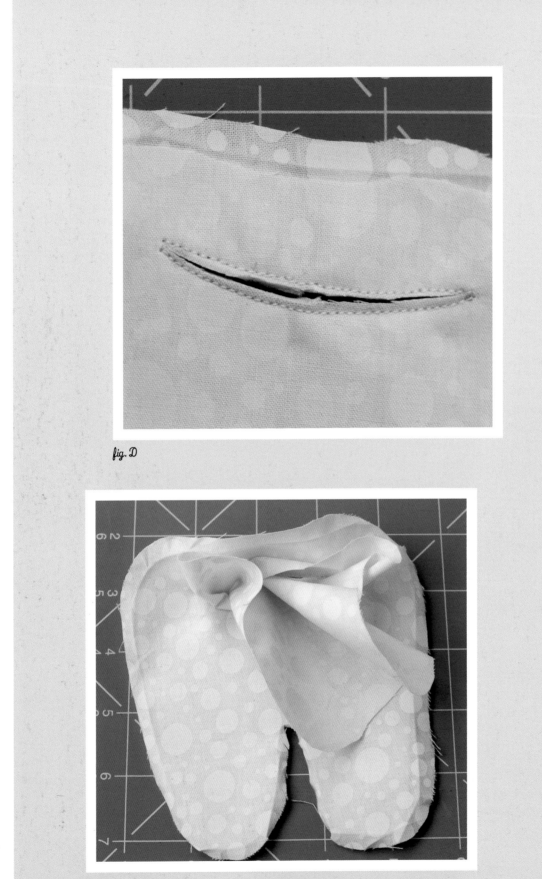

fig. D

fig. E

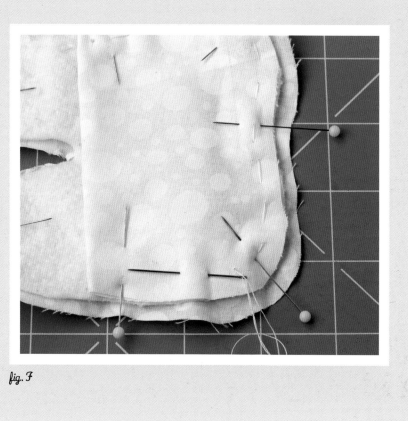

fig. F

❾ Transfer the smile motif onto the wrong side of the fabric C piece and then pin it to the large tooth set aside in step 5, right sides together. Stitch approximately ⅛ inch (3 mm) around the smile motif, pivoting at the corners. Open up the stitched smile using a sharp craft knife to carefully slice through all the fabric layers **(fig. D)**.

❿ Push the C layer of the fabric through the sliced hole. Pull the fabric all the way to the other side and press with an iron. Add a running stitch around the outside perimeter of the smile with perle cotton **(fig. E)**.

⓫ Fold the C layer of the fabric in half, up to the top of the tooth. Baste the B tooth fabric to the batting and the folded C fabric layer, making sure that the batting and folded fabric get neatly tucked beneath the seam allowance of the B tooth fabric **(fig. F)**.

⓬ Center the tooth onto the pillowcase and blind stitch in place. Quilt along the inside edge of the tooth with perle cotton. Echo quilt two rows of running stitches along the outside edges of the tooth.

⓭ Use a stem stitch and metallic embroidery floss to embroider a sparkle motif at the top right corner of the center tooth.

variation!
Appliqué these tooth motifs to a little quilt, and hang it off the headboard of your child's bed.

woodsy
GNOME DOLL

This chunky, bearded doll is so fun to make you may not be able to stop with just one.

from your stash

1 piece of drill fabric, 12 x 12 inches (30.5 x 30.5 cm)

1 piece of drill fabric, 4 x 5 inches (10.2 x 12.7 cm)

1 piece of scrap fabric, 12 x 12 inches (30.5 x 30.5 cm), plus additional scraps

Assorted felt scraps

Embroidery floss or perle cotton in assorted colors

gather

Basic appliqué sewing tool kit (page 7)

Templates (page 124)

Polyester fiberfill

1 piece of nonwoven medium-weight interfacing, 4 x 5 inches (10.2 x 12.7 cm)

make

❶ Cut out template A and trace it once onto the large piece of drill and once onto the large piece of scrap fabric to make the opposite pair. Cut out the shapes to create the front and back sides of the doll.

❷ Cut out templates B, C, D, E, F, G, and H and trace them onto assorted scraps of felt and fabric. Cut two of template H for the shoes. Arrange these pieces as desired, making sure that you have cut out all the parts and pieces needed (the face will be on the surface of the drill). Set aside **(fig. A)**.

TIP
Use the templates just the way they are (do not enlarge) and make a slightly smaller doll. Enlarge the templates by 200% to make a larger doll.

fig. A

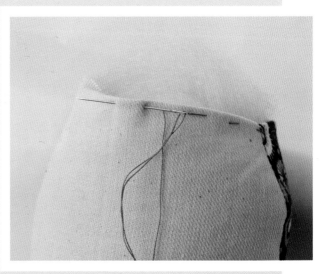

fig. B

fig. C

fig. D

3 Pin and stitch together the front and back of the doll, right sides together, using a ¼-inch (6 mm) seam allowance and leaving the bottom edge open. Cut notches along the curves and tip. Turn right side out.

4 Stuff with polyester fiberfill, using a pointy utensil as needed to stuff the points and curves. Avoid puckers by not overstuffing the doll.

5 Turn under the bottom edge of the sewn and stuffed doll by ¼ inch (6 mm) and baste to secure **(fig. B)**.

6 Cut template I and trace it once onto the remaining piece of drill and once onto the piece of interfacing. Cut out the shapes. Trim down the interfacing an extra ¼ inch (6 mm) so that it is slightly smaller than the oval drill.

7 Pin and stitch the interfacing oval onto the top of the drill oval, close to the edge of the interfacing.

8 Insert the stitched oval base into the opening at the base of the doll, hiding the interfacing inside, and blindstitch in place **(fig. C)**.

appliqué

9 Appliqué the pants set aside in step 2 onto the doll with embroidery floss, using an overcast stitch. Appliqué the shirt, beard, hair, shoes, and hat using an overcast stitch, overlapping each piece just slightly **(fig. D)**.

10 Cut a fabric scrap to measure 1 x 5¼ inches (2.5 x 13.3 cm) for the belt. Fold in each long side by ¼ inch (6 mm). Slip the belt buckle set aside in step 2 onto the belt. Pin the belt to the waist and overcast stitch in place.

11 Cut circles from felt scraps in desired sizes for the eyes and hat and overcast stitch in place. Embroider the mouth using an embroidery needle and brown embroidery floss. Add French knots to the center of the circles on the hat and to the ends of the mouth.

fun & friendly
FUROSHIKI

Make your own version of a furoshiki, a traditional Japanese wrapping cloth, for an elegant and creative way to brighten any gift presentation.

from your stash

1 piece of fabric,
24 x 24 inches (61 x 61 cm),
or size to fit your gift

1 piece of fabric for
binding, 1¼ x 108 inches
(3.2 x 274.3 cm)

Assorted fabric scraps

Perle cotton

gather

Basic appliqué sewing kit
(page 7)

Templates (page 126)

Paper-backed fusible web

make

1 Center the item you plan to wrap diagonally on the fabric and tie opposite corners of the fabric into half knots at the top of the item. Sew large basting stitches to mark the front, back, and sides (**fig. A**).

2 Untie the fabric and lay it flat. The basting stitches will form a cross that marks the bottom and sides of the item so that you can appropriately position the appliqué circle pieces.

3 Press a piece of the fusible web onto the back sides of the assorted fabric scraps.

4 Cut out the circle templates and trace them onto the paper side of the fused fabrics. Cut out the shapes. Peel off the paper backing, stack the circles as desired, and position the stacks onto the fabric so that all sides of the basted cross have stacked circles on them. The edges of some circles can overlap the lines. Press the stacked circles to the main fabric (**fig. B**).

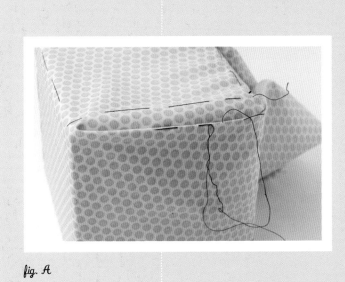

fig. A

fig. B

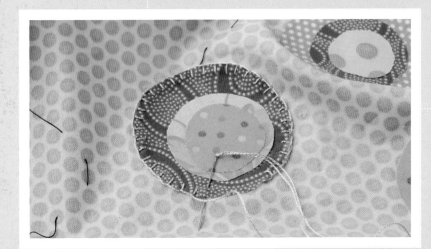

fig. C

fig. D

fig. E

fig. F

5 Embroider the fused circles with perle cotton using a blanket stitch, French knots, and other decorative stitches **(fig. C)**.

6 Use the binding technique found in the Basics section (page 12–13) to bind the main fabric with the binding fabric.

7 Add a decorative blanket stitch around the binding, using an embroidery needle and perle cotton **(fig. D)**.

finish

8 Rewrap your item, following the instructions in step 1, and remove the basting stitches **(figs. E-F)**.

TIP

After appliquéing all the circles on the cloth, cut out another cloth the same size and sew the pieces together around the outer edge, wrong sides together, then bind the cloth. This makes a reversible furoshiki.

floating heart ORNAMENT

With the help of a small piece of transparency, this stitched heart appears to float, making a truly magical ornament for hearth and home.

from your stash

1 piece of fabric, 2¼ x ¼ inches (5.7 cm x 6 mm)

Assorted fabric scraps

Scraps of batting

Perle cotton

Scrap of ribbon

gather

Basic appliqué sewing kit (page 7)

Templates (page 127)

Permanent black marker

Seed beads

Beading needle

1 piece of transparency, 4 x 4 inches (10.2 x 10.2 cm)

Glass ornament, 8½ inch (21.6 cm) circumference

Spray paint, or acrylic paint and paintbrush (optional)

make

❶ Cut out templates A (large), B (medium), and C (small) and trace each onto assorted fabric scraps. Cut out the shapes.

❷ Trace template C onto a scrap of batting using the permanent black marker. Cut along the inside of the marked line to create a piece of heart-shaped batting slightly smaller than the small fabric heart cut in step 1. Adhere the wrong side of the small fabric heart to the batting using spray adhesive **(fig. A)**.

❸ Adhere the large fabric heart onto a scrap of batting using spray adhesive and trim, leaving a tiny bit of the batting exposed **(fig. B)**.

❹ Make a sandwich with the small heart, medium heart (without batting), and the large heart, using spray adhesive **(fig. C)**. Overcast stitch around the perimeter of the small and medium hearts through all layers with a double strand of sewing thread **(fig. D)**.

❺ Attach small seed beads to the smallest heart as desired, using a beading needle and sewing thread.

fig. A

fig. B

fig. C

fig. D

fig. E

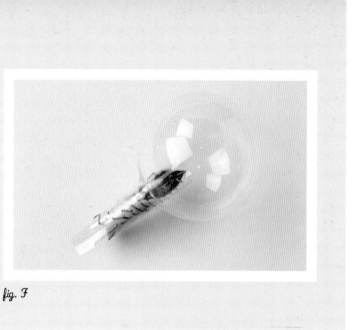

fig. F

❻ Cut out and trace template D onto a piece of transparency, using the permanent black marker. Cut out the transparency just inside the marked line and check to make sure it is slightly smaller than the ornament.

❼ Adhere the stitched heart to the cut transparency using spray adhesive. Overcast stitch the heart to the transparency using an embroidery needle and perle cotton **(fig. E)**.

finish

❽ Roll the stitched piece and carefully insert it into the glass ornament. Allow the piece to unfurl inside the ornament **(fig. F)**.

❾ Paint the lid of the ornament using spray paint or acrylic paint, or glue a strip of fabric around the top. Tie a piece of ribbon into a bow at the very top.

spring flowers
ZIP POUCH

The perfect little place to store
your small stuff.

from your stash

1 piece of fabric for front panel, 5½ x 10⅛ inches (14 x 25.7 cm)

1 piece of fabric for back panel, 7 x 10⅛ inches (17.8 x 25.7 cm)

2 pieces of fabric for lining, each 7 x 10⅛ inches (17.8 x 25.7 cm)

7 pieces of fabric in coordinating colors, each 1¾ x 1¾ inches (4.4 x 4.4 cm)

1 piece of fabric for zipper stop, 1 x 1 inch (2.5 x 2.5 cm)

1 piece of fabric for zipper pull, 1½ x 7 inches (3.8 x 17.8 cm)

Assorted fabric scraps

2 pieces of batting, each 7 x 10½ inches (17.8 x 26.7 cm)

gather

Basic appliqué sewing tool kit (page 7)

Templates (page 125)

¼ yard (.23 m) of paper-backed fusible web

Zipper foot

1 zipper, 9 inches (22.8 cm) long

2 pieces of single-fold bias tape, each 6½ inches (16.5 cm) long

make

① Cut out the templates and trace them onto the paper side of the fusible web. Press the fusible web onto the wrong sides of the fabric scraps and trace the shapes. Be sure to trace the stems onto the same fabric scraps, and flowers onto different fabric scraps. Cut out the shapes and set aside.

② Stitch together two of the fabric squares, right sides together, along one edge using a ¼-inch (6 mm) seam allowance. In like fashion, stitch a third square along the opposite edge of one of the joined squares. Continue stitching squares to form a patchwork strip with all seven fabric squares. Press all the seams in one direction.

③ Stitch the patchwork strip to the bottom of the front panel fabric, using a ¼-inch (6 mm) seam allowance. Press the seam allowance toward the front panel. True up the sides of the patchwork panel if necessary.

④ Arrange the appliqué pieces on the front panel, keeping the A pieces, B pieces, and C pieces together. Peel off the paper backing and fuse with an iron. Overcast stitch all of the fused appliqué pieces with thread to secure (fig. A).

fig. A

stitch the bag

⑤ Baste the front panel to one of the batting pieces and the back panel fabric to the remaining batting piece.

⑥ Stitch the zipper stop fabric onto the end of the zipper using a ¼-inch (6 mm) seam allowance. Trim down the zipper to meet the edge of the fabric.

⑦ Fold under the zipper stop fabric by ¼ inch (6 mm) and stitch to secure.

⑧ Attach the zipper foot to your sewing machine and left align the needle. Sew the front panel to one edge of the zipper and the back panel to the opposite edge of the zipper, right sides together **(fig. B)**.

⑨ Place the right side of one of the lining pieces to the wrong side of the zipper and stitch. During this process, you may need to position the needle down and carefully move the zipper pull as you continue stitching. Repeat with the remaining lining piece and the opposite side of the zipper. At this point you have sandwiched the zipper between the lining and the outer pouch.

⑩ Lay the pouch flat and topstitch the front and back panels near the top edge **(fig. C)**.

⑪ Pin the lining pieces, right sides together. Stitch the bottom seam using a 1¼-inch (6 mm) seam allowance. Repeat for the outer pouch.

⑫ Turn the pouch inside out. Stitch together the side seams, right sides together **(fig. D)**.

bind

⑬ Stitch one piece of single-fold bias tape onto one side edge of the lining using a straight stitch. Turn the binding up and over to encase the seam and then secure using a zigzag stitch. Repeat with the remaining piece of binding on the other side of the lining. Turn the pouch right side out **(fig. E)**.

⑭ Fold under all sides of the zipper pull fabric by ¼ inch (6 mm) and topstitch to secure. Loop the fabric through the zipper and tie a knot to secure it onto the zipper pull.

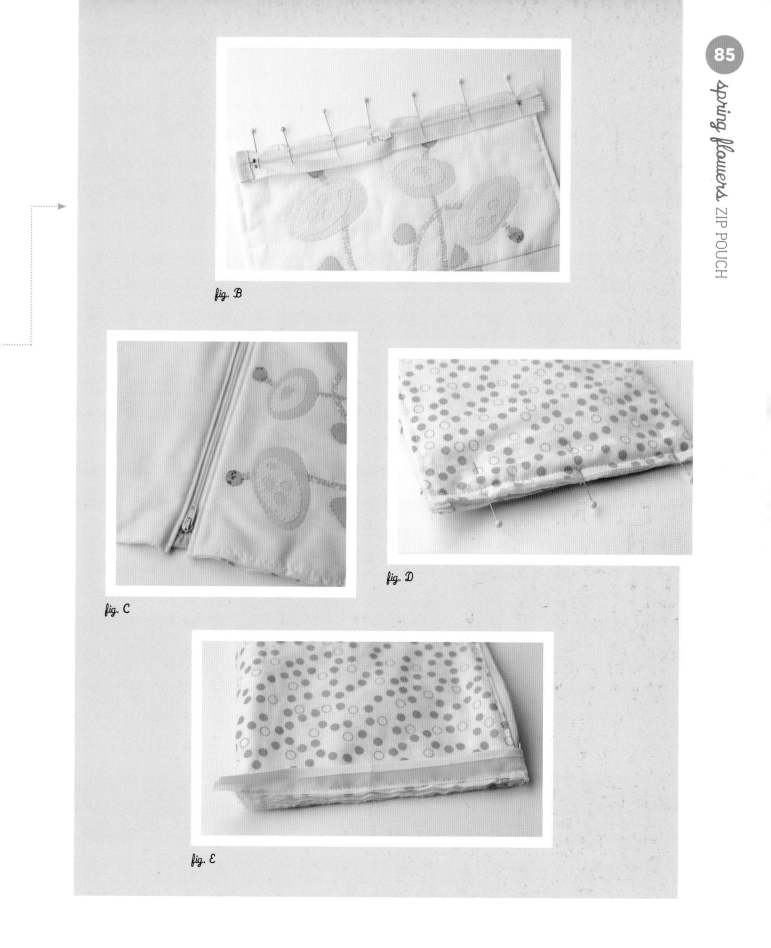

fig. B

fig. C

fig. D

fig. E

everyday
MOD SKIRT

Whether you're headed to school or to work or to play, this skirt will become your go-to favorite.

from your stash

1 piece of blue jersey for outer skirt, 41 x 21 inches (104.1 x 53.3 cm)

1 piece of teal jersey for underskirt, 41 x 21 inches (104.1 x 53.3 cm)

1 scrap of white jersey for appliqué

1 piece of green jersey, ³⁄₈ x 30 inches (9.5 mm x 76.2 cm), plus scrap for appliqué

1 piece of blue jersey for waistband, 2¾ x 32 inches (7 x 81.2 cm)

1 piece of teal jersey for casing, 1½ x 54 (3.8 x 137.2 cm)

Perle cotton

gather

Basic appliqué sewing kit (page 7)

Templates (page 126)

54 inches (137.16 cm) of drawstring cording

make

❶ Fold the outer skirt fabric in half lengthwise, right sides together, and stitch together the long edge using a ½-inch (1.3 cm) seam allowance. In like fashion stitch together the underskirt fabric. Press the seams of both tubes open.

❷ Drop the underskirt tube into the outer skirt tube with the right side of the underskirt facing the wrong side of the outer skirt. Baste the top edge in place using a ½-inch (1.3 cm) seam allowance.

❸ Draw a line on the outer skirt, parallel to and 4¼ inches (10.8 cm) from the bottom edge, using a washable fabric marker.

❹ Lay the skirt flat and thoroughly pin the outer and under layers of the skirt at multiple points. Hand-baste staystitches (a single line of stitching to stabilize the fabric) at the bottom edge, the drawn line, and 4 inches (10.2 cm) above the line **(fig. A)**.

fig. A

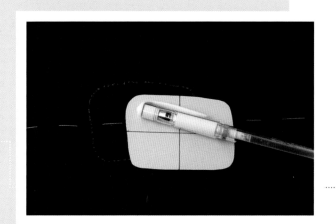

fig. B

fig. C

fig. D

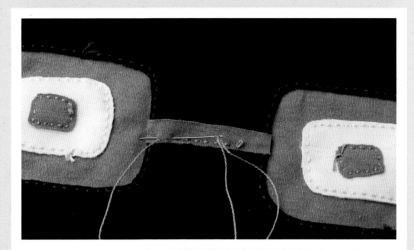

fig. E

appliqué

5 Cut out template A and trace it around the outer skirt at the drawn line, evenly spaced, using a washable fabric marker. You will trace the shape eight times **(fig. B)**.

6 Backstitch the skirt layers at one of the traced A shapes using an embroidery needle and perle cotton so that the stitches are slightly outside of the pencil line. Cut open the outer skirt layer to reveal the underskirt **(fig. C)**.

7 Cut out template B, trace it eight times onto white fabric, and cut them out.

8 Adhere a white jersey piece onto the revealed underskirt using spray adhesive. Backstitch around the edges, leaving the knots exposed **(fig. D)**. Cut out template C and trace it eight times onto the green scrap and cut out. In like fashion, appliqué a green jersey piece onto the white piece you just stitched. Repeat steps with the remaining shapes along the entire skirt. Remove all staystitches.

9 Measure the distance between two white appliqué shapes. Cut a piece of green jersey to this length and adhere it to the outer skirt using spray adhesive, joining the two appliqués. Backstitch the edges with perle cotton, leaving knots exposed. Repeat to join the remaining appliqués with strips of green jersey along the entire outer skirt **(fig. E)**.

finish the skirt

10 Fold the waistband fabric lengthwise, right sides together, to form a closed loop. Stitch the short raw edges using a ½-inch (1.3 cm) seam allowance; begin at the bottom edge and stitch ½ inch (1.3 cm), backstitching, leaving ¾ inch (1.9 cm) unstitched, backstitch, and then stitch the remainder of the seam. The unstitched section creates an opening for the drawstring cording.

11 Press the seam allowance open and stitch it down on both sides of the opening.

12 Pin one long edge of the waistband to the outer skirt, right sides together, with the opening for the drawstring cording centered at the front of the skirt. Stretch the layers and pin the back seam, then the front seam, and then the midpoints between the front and back seams. Stretch and pin between these pinned spots, easing the skirt onto the waistband. Stitch together using a ½-inch (1.3 cm) seam allowance **(fig. F)**.

13 Fold the waistband to the inside of the skirt and pin in place, overlapping the waist seam by ½ inch (1.3 cm). Do not turn under the edge. Finish by stitching in the ditch, on the outer skirt.

14 Fold under the outer skirt hem 1 inch (2.5 cm) and backstitch in place, exposing the knots. Then fold up the underskirt hem ½ inch (1.3 cm) and backstitch in place.

15 Remove all the basting stitches.

16 Fold the casing fabric around the drawstring cording and sew all edges closed with perle cotton, using a straight stitch. Attach a safety pin at one end of the cording and push it into the hole at the front waistband seam, work it all the way through, and pull it back out through the opposite hole at the front waistband seam.

fig. F

angel wings
ALTERED TEE

Calling all angels: Your wings are here!

from your stash

¼ yard (.23 m) of pink fabric

¼ yard (.23 m) of white fabric

1 piece of batting, 10 x 10 inches (25.4 x 25.4 cm)

Embroidery floss in dark and light pink

gather

Basic appliqué sewing kit (page 7)

Templates (page 126)

½ yard (.5 m) paper-backed fusible web

T-shirt

make

1 Cut out templates A (large wing) and B (small wing). Trace them each onto the paper side of the fusible web, then flip them over to trace a second time as a mirror image.

2 Press the large wing shapes onto the wrong side of the pink fabric and the small wing shapes onto the wrong side of the white fabric. Cut out the shapes.

3 Peel off the paper backings and press the pink wings as desired onto the T-shirt. Then peel off the paper backings and press the white wings onto the piece of batting and cut out the white wings.

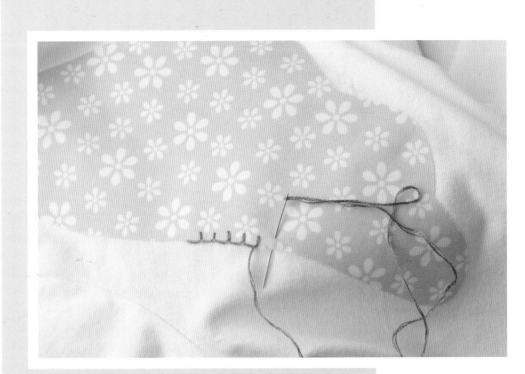

fig. A

fig. B

④ Embroider the pink wings using a blanket stitch and dark pink embroidery floss **(fig. A)**.

⑤ Adhere the white wings onto the pink wings using spray adhesive. Embroider the white wings using a blanket stitch and light pink embroidery floss **(fig. B)**.

variation!

Create a parent and child set of winged tees by enlarging the templates to better fit an adult-sized shirt.

your house
HOOP ART

Re-create a photograph for a
one-of-a-kind housewarming gift.

from your stash

1 piece of muslin, 12 x 12 inches
(30.5 x 30.5 cm)

Assorted fabric scraps

Embroidery floss in
coordinating colors

gather

Basic appliqué sewing kit
(page 7)

Computer-generated color
printout of a house image, 5 x 7
inches (12.7 x 17.8 cm)

Wooden embroidery hoop, 8
inches (20.3 cm) in diameter

make

1 Isolate the house from the background by cutting away excess or
unnecessary portions of the image.

2 Outline the shape of the embroidery hoop on the muslin, using a
washable fabric marker, to serve as a guide for where to appliqué.

3 Place the cutout house onto the right side of the fabric scrap you've
chosen to be the main fabric in this project. Trace the shape, and cut it
out. All the other pieces of fabric will be appliquéd onto this main fabric
piece **(fig. A)**.

4 Cut out a portion of the house from the printout and place it onto the
right side of a second fabric scrap and cut out the shape **(fig. B)**.

fig. A

fig. B

fig. C

fig. D

⑤ Continue isolating other portions of the house, such as the chimney, doors, and windows. Cut out the desired portions from the image, trace them onto fabric scraps, and cut out the shapes.

⑥ Adhere all the cut fabric pieces to the main house fabric as desired to create the house, using spray adhesive. Stitch all pieces in place. For the front door, add extra stitching using a sewing machine and white thread **(fig. C)**.

⑦ Cut additional fabric scraps to add trees, shrubs, and other details. Adhere in place using spray adhesive and stitch in place.

finish

⑧ Add French knots, embroider the street address, and add other decorative details as desired, using an embroidery needle and floss **(fig. D)**.

⑨ Secure the embroidery hoop onto the finished appliqué and trim any excess muslin close to the edge of the hoop. Apply a small amount of fray retardant along the raw edge of the muslin to prevent fraying.

afield & aflutter TRENCHCOAT

Breathe new life into a classic trench coat with appliquéd bursts of color on its lapels. While you're adding color, cover the coat's buttons to match. So cute!

from your stash

Purple butterfly motif fabric scrap

Pink fabric scrap with butterfly (or other) motif

Solid purple fabric scrap

Embroidery floss

Perle cotton

gather

Basic appliqué sewing kit (page 7)

Paper-backed fusible web, to fit the motif fabric scraps

Trenchcoat

make

① Press a piece of paper-backed fusible web onto the wrong sides of the motif fabric scraps. Cut out the butterfly shapes **(fig. A)**.

② Peel off the paper backing and arrange the motifs as desired on the trench coat lapels and collar, and pin in place. Place a contrasting pink-colored fabric motif to add an unexpected color accent **(fig. B)**.

③ Use the iron to fuse each butterfly in place, removing pins as you go.

④ Stitch a quick overcast stitch around each butterfly, using an embroidery needle and floss.

⑤ Add a large, chunky running stitch along the edges of the lapels, using a double strand of perle cotton in a contrasting color **(fig. C)**.

fig. A

fig. B

fig. C

fig. D

cover the buttons

6 Remove all the buttons. Use coordinating scrap fabric to cut circles that measure twice the diameter of the buttons.

7 Sew a loose running stitch along the edge of each scrap fabric circle, using embroidery needle and thread, and then gently pull the thread to cinch up the circle **(fig. D)**.

8 Place a button in the center of each cinched circle and fully draw up the fabric. Stitch each circle closed with multiple back-and-forth stitches.

9 Stitch the buttons back onto the trench using a double strand of perle cotton in a contrasting color.

mom & daughter
APRON SET

This apron is so cute you'll be tempted to keep it on long after the cookies have been baked and the kitchen has been cleaned!

from your stash (for the adult)

1 piece of dark-colored fabric, 6 x 10 inches (15.2 x 25.4 cm)

1 piece of fabric for pocket panel, 19 x 7½ inches (48.3 x 19 cm)

1 piece of fabric for apron panel, 19 x 14 inches (48.3 x 35.6 cm)

2 pieces of cream-colored fabric for ties, each 2½ x 36 inches (6.4 x 91.4 cm)

1 piece of cream-colored fabric for waistband, 4 x 14½ inches (10.2 x 36.8 cm)

1 piece of bias-cut accent fabric, 1½ x 35 inches (3.8 x 89 cm)

gather

Basic appliqué sewing kit (page 7)

Templates (page 121)

1 piece of paper-backed fusible web, 6 x 10 inches (15.2 x 25.4 cm)

20 inches (50.8 cm) of double-fold bias tape

50 inches (127 cm) of extra-wide double-fold bias tape

1 piece of lightweight interfacing, 2 x 14½ inches (5.1 x 36.8 cm)

from your stash (for the child)

1 piece of dark-colored fabric, 5 x 5 inches (12.7 x 12.7 cm)

1 piece of fabric for pocket panel, 14 x 5½ inches (35.6 x 14 cm)

1 piece of fabric for apron panel, 14 x 10 inches (35.6 x 25.4 cm)

2 pieces of cream-colored fabric for ties, each 2¼ x 30 inches (5.7 x 76.2 cm)

1 piece of cream-colored fabric for waistband, 3½ x 11 inches (8.9 x 27.9 cm)

1 piece of bias-cut accent fabric, 1 x 24 inches (2.5 x 61 cm)

gather

Basic appliqué sewing kit (page 7)

Templates (page 121)

1 piece of paper-backed fusible web, 5 x 5 inches (12.7 x 12.7 cm)

14 inches (35.6 cm) of double-fold bias tape

35 inches (89 cm) of extra-wide double-fold bias tape

1 piece of lightweight interfacing, 1¾ x 11 inches (4.4 x 27.9 cm)

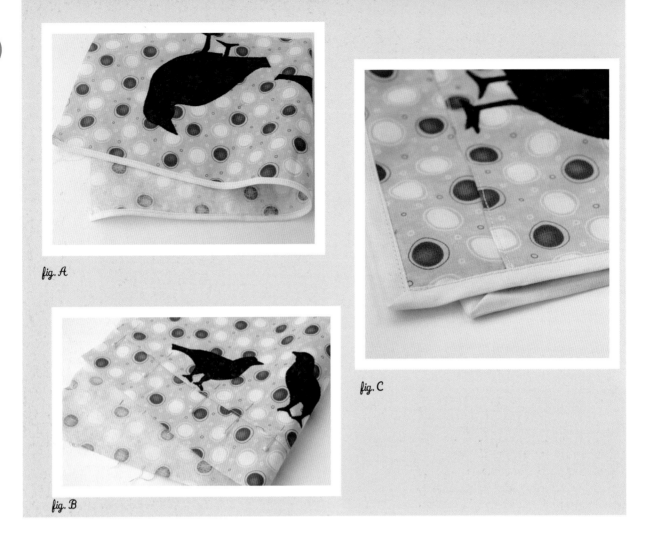

fig. A

fig. B

fig. C

make (adult's apron)

1 Cut out and trace right side of template A once and right side of template B twice onto the paper side of the fusible web. Flip the right side of the template facing the paper-backed fusible web.

2 Press the traced fusible web onto the wrong side of the dark-colored fabric and cut out the three birds. Set aside the fused scraps. Peel off the paper backing from the birds and fuse them onto the pocket panel as desired.

3 Stich an open zigzag stitch around the edges of all the birds.

stitch the apron
4 Stitch the double-fold bias tape onto the top edge of the pocket panel by first stitching along the right side of the panel. Flip the bias tape up, over, and around the raw panel edge, and then stitch the bias tape again from the right side of the panel **(fig. A)**.

5 Turn under the bottom edge of the pocket panel by ½ inch (1.3 cm) and press.

6 Pin the pocket panel to the apron panel, aligning side edges, and positioning the bottom edge of the pocket panel 2 inches (5.1 cm) above the bottom edge of the apron panel. Topstitch the folded bottom edge of the pocket panel, and then baste the sides **(fig. B)**.

7 Fold the apron in half widthwise and press lightly to find the center. Stitch down the center of the pocket panel to create two pockets, stopping and starting as necessary to avoid stitching across the bird appliqué. Backtack at the start and end to secure the thread.

8 Use the binding techniques found in the Basics section (page 12–13) to bind the sides and bottom of the apron, using the extra-wide double-fold bias tape **(fig. C)**.

fig. D

stitch the waistband

9 Place pins at the top edge of the apron panel, one each 3½ inches (8.9 cm) from the outer edges, and one each 6½ inches (16.5 cm) from the outer edges. Create ¾-inch (1.9 cm) tucks at each of these points and push those tucks toward the center of the apron panel. Baste across the top edge, removing the pins that hold the tucks in place **(fig. D)**.

10 Fold under the two lengthwise edges and one width edge of a piece of tie fabric by ¼ inch (6 mm), then fold under the edges another ¼ inch (6 mm). Sew continuously around the three sides of the tie, leaving one raw width edge. Repeat this step for the second tie.

11 Fuse the lightweight fusible interfacing to the wrong side of the waistband fabric, aligning top edges. Press the unfused waistband edge up by ½ inch (1.3 cm).

12 Pin the ties to the fused waistband, with raw edges aligned and right sides together. The lower edge of the tie should align with the pressed line along the waistband. Fold the waistband along this line to sandwich the ties inside the fold. Stitch together the width edges using a ½-inch (1.3 cm) seam allowance **(fig. E)**.

fig. E

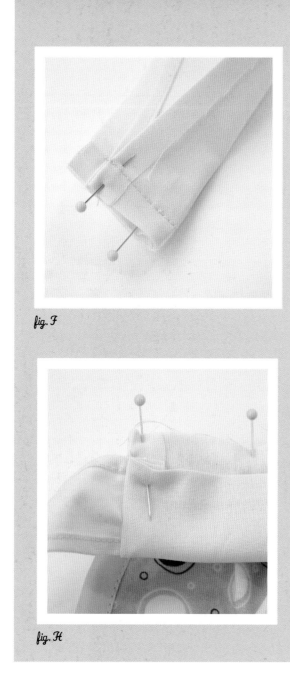

fig. F

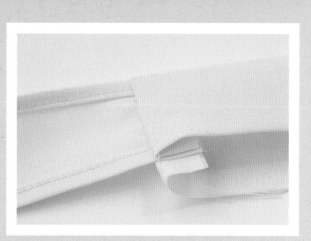

fig. G

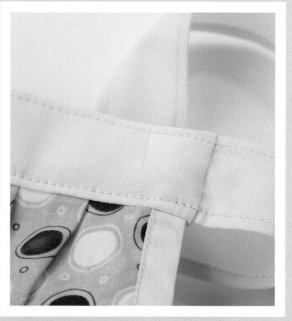

fig. I

fig. H

⑬ Clip the corners and turn right side out **(figs. F–G)**.

⑭ Pin the waistband onto the apron, with raw edges aligned and right sides together, and stitch across, being careful to avoid stitching the folded-up section of the waistband **(fig. H).**

⑮ Fold over the waistband and pin the inside of the waistband to the wrong side of the apron. Topstitch the top and bottom of the waistband **(fig. I).**

finish

⑯ Stitch a gathering stitch along the center of the accent fabric. Pull the threads to create a ruffle and pin the fabric to the bottom section of the apron, just above the binding. Fold under both ends and stitch.

⑰ Cut three circles that measure 1 inch (2.5 cm), ⅞ inch (2.2 cm), and ¾ inch (1.9 cm) in diameter, respectively, from the fused fabric set aside in step 2.

⑱ Peel off the paper backing and fuse the dots to the waistband as desired. Stitch an open zigzag stitch along around the edges of the dots.

make (child's apron)

1 Follow steps 1–16 to make an apron for a child, using the measurements and seam allowances instructed for the adult-size apron. Instead of cutting three template shapes, only cut one of template B.

2 Cut three circles that measure ¾ inch (1.9 cm), ⅝ inch (1.6 cm), and ½ inch (1.3 cm) in diameter, respectively, from the fused fabric set aside in step 2 of the instructions.

3 Peel off the paper backing and fuse the dots to the waistband as desired. Stitch an open zigzag stitch around the edges of the dots.

variation!

Make your own custom bias tape from fun patterned fabric by following the directions on page 12.

kid art
TRIPTYCH

The next time your child creates a masterpiece, transform it into a sewn work of art.

from your stash

Fabric scraps in coordinating colors

3 pieces of white linen fabric, each 10 x 10 inches (25.4 x 25.4 cm)

3 pieces of batting, each 10 x 10 inches (25.4 x 25.4 cm)

Embroidery floss in two coordinating colors

gather

Basic appliqué sewing kit (page 7)

Color copy of three pieces of original art

Fine-point permanent black marker

¼ yard (.23 m) of paper-backed fusible web

Masking tape

3 stretched canvases, each 6 x 6 inches (15.2 x 15.2 cm)

Staple gun

Mounting hardware for the canvases

prepare

This project uses art made by my son when he was a little boy. The art that your child makes will be different and will affect the types of fabric you select and the specific ways you'll need to create your appliqué. Please take the basic principles I offer here and tailor them to suit the unique details of the art that you choose.

make

❶ Outline the shapes of the color copy using a permanent marker **(fig. A)**.

❷ Place the paper-backed fusible web onto the outlined art, with the web side facing the art. Trace the parts and pieces of the art that will be used to create the appliqué. For my son's art, I decided to make the face, the inner eyes, and the spots on the body in green, so I traced those parts in one cluster and the remaining parts of the art in a second cluster.

❸ Press the traced fusible web onto the wrong sides of the coordinating fabric scraps and cut out the shapes **(fig. B)**. For this project, the fainter wrong side of the green fabric was used as the right side.

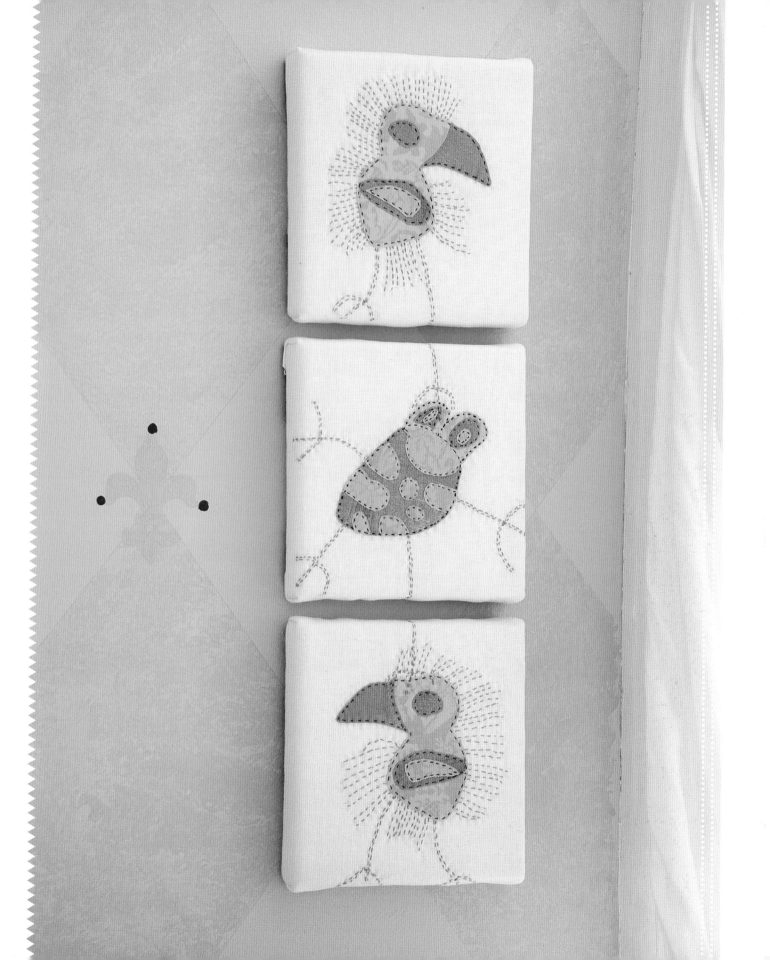

fig. A

fig. B

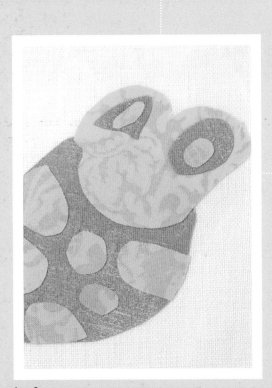

fig. C

fig. D

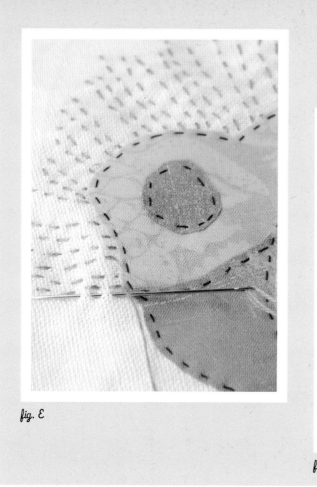

fig. E

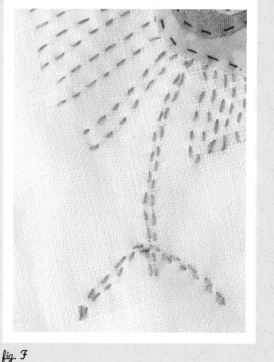

fig. F

④ Mark a square that measures 6 x 6 inches (15.2 x 15.2 cm) onto one piece of white linen fabric, using a washable fabric marker.

appliqué

⑤ Fuse the cut shapes of fabric onto the marked white fabric, centered, to re-create the artwork **(fig. C)**.

⑥ Hand-sew a running stitch along all the edges of all appliqued pieces, using an embroidery needle and a double strand of black sewing thread **(fig. D)**. Fill in the rest of the figure with running stitches using coordinating colors of embroidery floss **(fig. E)**.

⑦ Adhere the white fabric to one piece of cut batting, using spray adhesive. Sew a running stitch around the perimeter with white thread, ⅛ inch (3 mm) away from the shape.

⑧ Embroider the legs with two different colors of embroidery floss. Sew a running stitch around the embroidered legs with white thread **(fig. F)**.

⑨ Tape the work onto one stretched canvas and secure it in place using a staple gun. Remove the tape.

⑩ Repeat steps 1–9 using two additional pieces of art and mount the canvases in a playful fashion onto the wall.

variation!

Transfer the shape of the child's art onto a T-shirt and applique a unique wearable to present as a gift for the doting grandma or grandpa.

carried away
TOTE BAG

Carry your every day
necessities with style.

from your stash

²/₃ yard (.6 m) of linen

½ yard (.5 m) of lining fabric

1 piece of pocket fabric,
7 x 7 inches (17.8 x 17.8 cm)

1 piece of fabric for the belt
loops, 1⅞ x 10 inches
(4.8 x 25.4 cm)

1 piece of fabric for the sash,
2¼ x 48 inches (5.7 x 122 cm)

1 piece of fabric for the strap,
4 x 31 inches (10.2 x 78.7 cm)

Fabric scraps in assorted colors

gather

Basic appliqué sewing kit
(page 7)

Templates (page 118–119)

Freezer paper

Glue stick

½ yard (.5 m) of medium-weight
fusible interfacing

1 piece of medium-weight
fusible interfacing for the strap,
2 x 31 inches (5.1 x 78.7 cm)

make

❶ Cut out templates A, B, C, D, E, and F and trace them onto the dull side of
the freezer paper as follows:

A—Trace once
B—Trace twice, flipping over the template to trace it the second time
C—Trace twice, flipping over the template to trace it the second time
D—Trace twice, flipping over the template to trace it the second time
E—Trace once
F—Trace once

❷ Cut out the shapes and, with the shiny sides facing the fabric, press the
shapes onto the wrong side of the scrap fabrics. Cut out the fabric shapes,
allowing an extra ¼ inch (6 mm) of fabric to extend past the freezer
paper edges.

❸ Apply glue to the outer edges of the freezer paper and the fabric allowance
on one of the cut fabric shapes. Start at the tip of the shape and fold over the
fabric, adhering it to the freezer paper. Work around the entire shape, clipping
at the curves and applying more glue as needed. Repeat this step for all the
appliqué pieces **(fig. A)**.

❹ Cut out template G and pin and trace it onto the linen twice. Cut out the
shapes. Repeat to pin, trace, and cut out template G pieces from the lining
fabric and medium-weight fusible interfacing. Transfer all markings from the
template as follows:

fig. A

fig. B

Front linen piece—On the right side, transfer belt loop placements.

Front lining piece—On the wrong side, transfer tuck marks.

Back linen piece—On the right side, transfer belt loop placements.

Back lining piece—On the right side, mark the pocket placement. On the wrong side, transfer tuck marks.

Front and back interfacing pieces—On the nonfusible sides, transfer tuck marks.

❺ Fold and crease a vertical center line on the front linen piece. Fold and crease the bottom edge by ½ inch (1.3 cm) above the square-shaped cutouts. Fold and crease a line along the bottom belt loop marks, so that you do not appliqué the motif beyond that line. Pin the appliquéd pieces to the front linen piece as shown and blind stitch in place, using a sewing needle and thread in a matching color **(fig. B)**.

❻ Cut a slit into the center of an appliquéd area from the back side of the linen and pull the freezer paper out. Repeat for all the appliquéd pieces.

stitch the bag

❼ Trim down the top edges of the interfacing pieces by ¼ inch (6 mm). Fuse the interfacing to the wrong sides of both the front and back linen pieces.

❽ Fold the fused front piece using the dot marks on the interfacing as a guide. Pin and stitch ¼ inch (6 mm) from the fold, starting at the top dot and ending at the bottom dot, using backtacks to secure the thread at both ends. Repeat this step to create four tucks, two on each side of the front, and press the tucks toward the center of the bag. Repeat step 9 to make four tucks on the fused back piece **(fig. C)**.

❾ Pin the front and back linen pieces, right sides together, using a ½-inch (1.3 cm) seam allowance. Stitch together the side and bottom seams, but do not stitch the cutouts on the bottom edge **(fig. D)**.

❿ Press open the side seams and the bottom seam. Pressing open the bottom seam is not an easy process but it is necessary.

⓫ Flatten the cutouts to make corners and stitch them using a ½–inch (1.3 cm) seam allowance **(fig. E)**.

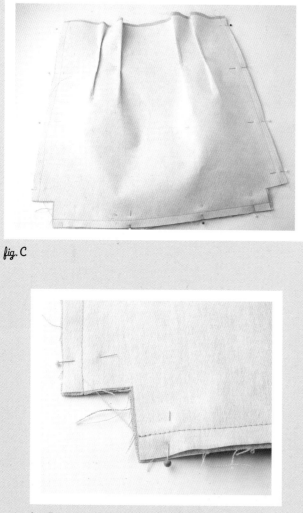

fig. C

fig. D

fig. E

stitch the pocket and lining

12 Press under the top edge of the pocket fabric by ¼ inch (6 mm). Press it back on itself by ¾ inch (1.9 cm). Stitch down the side edges using a ½-inch (1.3 cm) seam allowance **(fig. F)**.

13 Turn the flap up and over, which will cause the side seams to fold in by ½ inch (1.3 cm). Press the bottom edge to the wrong side of the pocket by ½ inch (1.3 cm). Stitch down the top flap **(fig. G)**.

14 Pin and stitch the pocket to the back lining piece, following the marks for pocket placement.

15 Repeat step 8 to create tucks for the front and back lining pieces. However, when pressing the tucks, press them toward the outer edges to reduce the bulk inside the bag.

16 Pin the lining pieces, right sides together, using a ½-inch (1.3 cm) seam allowance. Stitch together the side and bottom seams, leaving a 4-inch (10.2 cm) opening and backtacking at both ends of the opening to secure the stitches. Do not stitch the cutouts on the bottom edge. Press open the seams **(fig. H)**.

17 Flatten the cutouts to make corners and stitch them using a ½-inch (1.3 cm) seam allowance.

fig. G

fig. F

fig. H

assemble

⑱ Drop the linen bag into the lining with right sides together and top edges aligned. Stitch around the top of the bag using a ½-inch (1.3 cm) seam allowance **(fig. I)**.

fig. I

⑲ Turn the bag right side out through the opening at the bottom of the lining.

⑳ Fold in the edges of the opening and machine-stitch closed. Push the lining down into the bag.

㉑ Press the top edge of the bag and topstitch ¼ inch (6 mm) from the edge along the entire top of the bag **(fig. J)**.

fig. J

finish

22 Fold the belt loop fabric in half lengthwise, right sides together, and stitch using a ¼-inch (6 mm) seam allowance. Use a safety pin to turn the fabric right side out. Press and cut the fabric into four pieces, each 2½ inches (6.4 cm) long **(fig. K)**.

23 Turn under both ends of a belt loop and match it with a set of belt loop marks on the front of the bag. Pin in place with the loop pointing toward the top of the bag. Stitch the loop using a ¼-inch (6 mm) seam allowance. Repeat this step to secure the remaining belt loops to the bag **(fig. L)**.

24 Fold the sash fabric in half lengthwise, with right sides together, and stitch along the length using a ½-inch (1.3 cm) seam allowance. Use a safety pin to turn the fabric right side out, and press flat. Roll under the raw edges and whipstitch closed. Place the sash through the belt loops and tie into a bow.

25 Center the interfacing for the strap onto the wrong side of the strap fabric and press. Fold the strap fabric in half lengthwise, with right sides together, and stitch using a ½-inch (1.3 cm) seam allowance and leaving a 4-inch (10.2 cm) opening at the center. Clip the corners, turn right side out, and press. Fold in the edges of the opening and whipstitch closed.

26 Pin the strap to one side of the bag and stitch in place. Repeat to attach the other side of the strap to the opposite side of the bag.

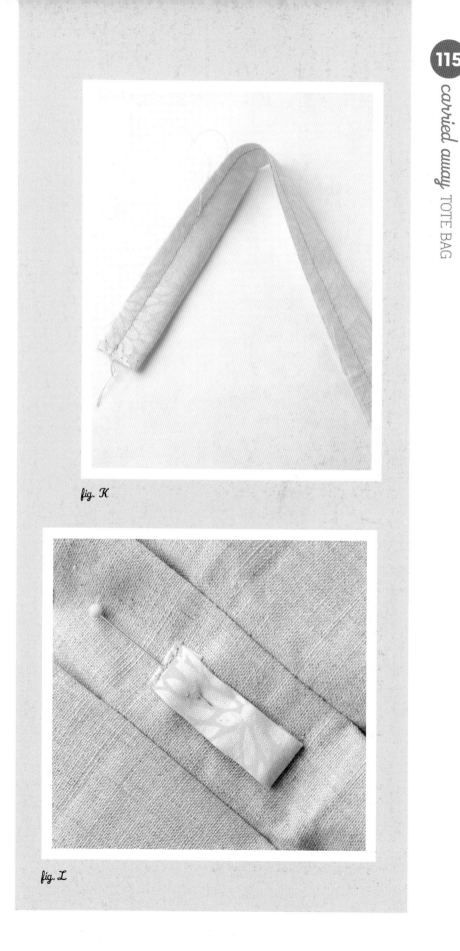

fig. K

fig. L

templates

sweet dreams tooth pillow, page 64
(enlarge 200%)

colorful & portable
tic-tac-toe, page 47

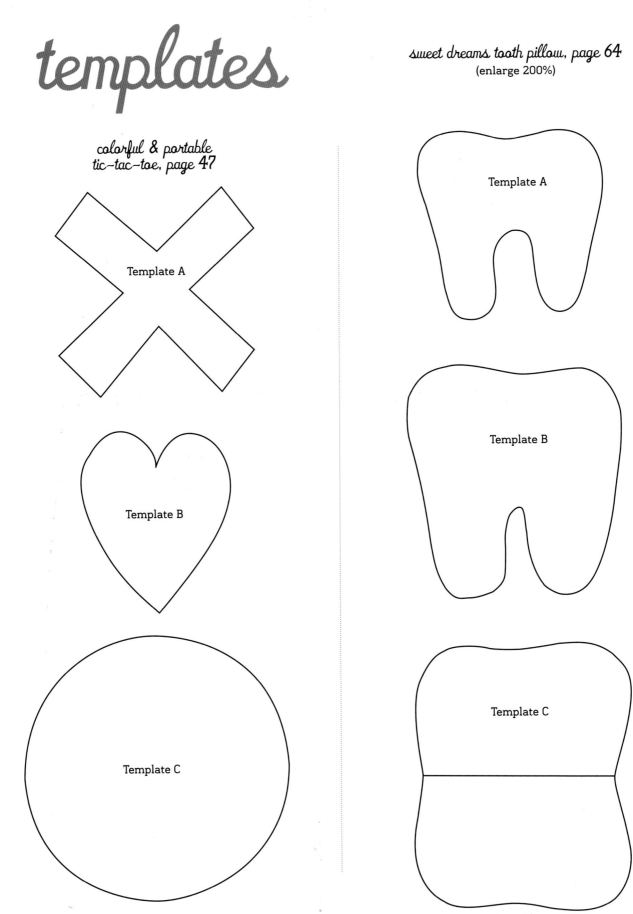

Template A

Template B

Template C

Template A

Template B

Template C

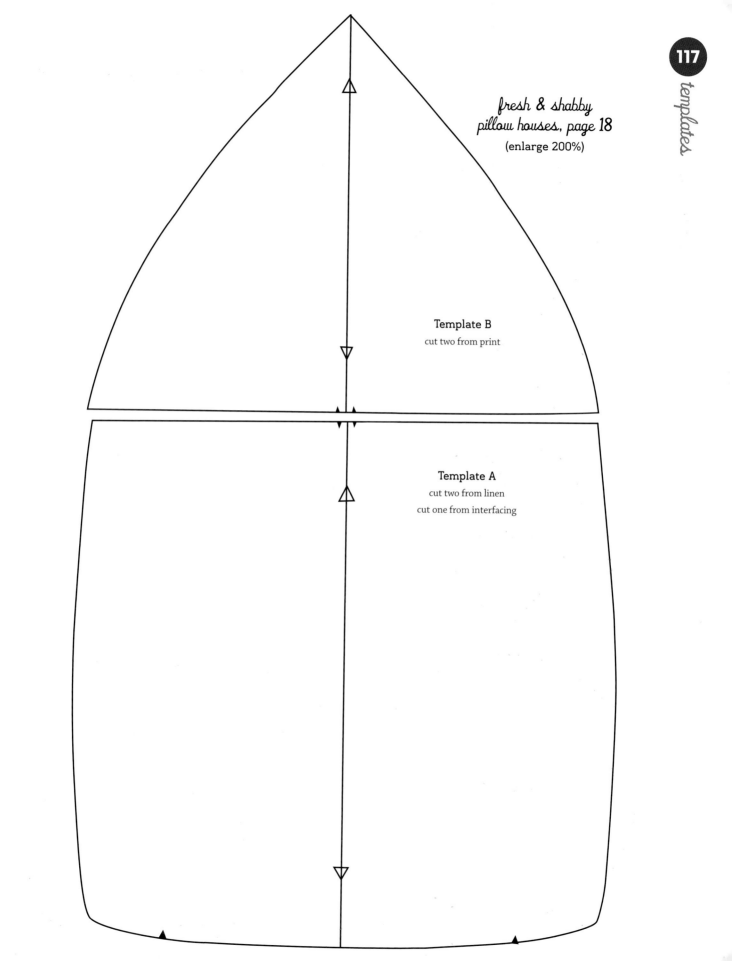

fresh & shabby
pillow houses, page 18
(enlarge 200%)

Template B
cut two from print

Template A
cut two from linen
cut one from interfacing

dream big! banner, page 56
(enlarge 200%)

d r   m b

e a i g !

carried away tote bag, page 110
(enlarge 250%)

A   B   C   D   E   F

carried away tote bag, page 110
(enlarge 250%)

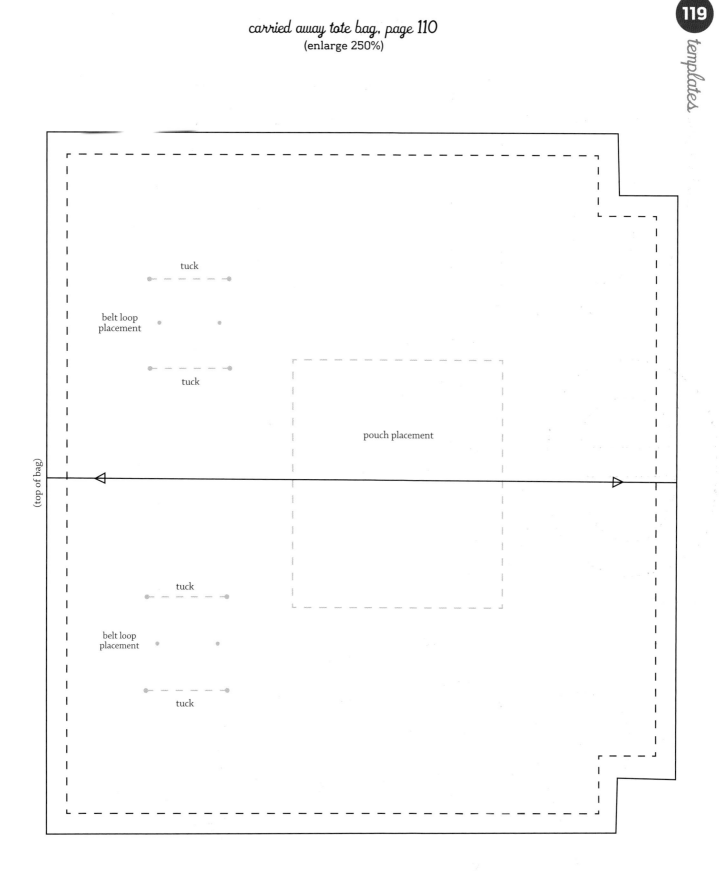

flower power pendant,
page 37

little miss mason jars, page 40

modern mary janes, page 23

no time like the present
play watch, page 60

A

B

C

pretty little paisley brooch,
page 44

A

B

C

mom & daughter apron set, page 100

Template A

Template B

scrappy & scrumptious
mug rugs, page 14
(enlarge 200%)

Template A

Template B

sail away baby ensemble, page 52

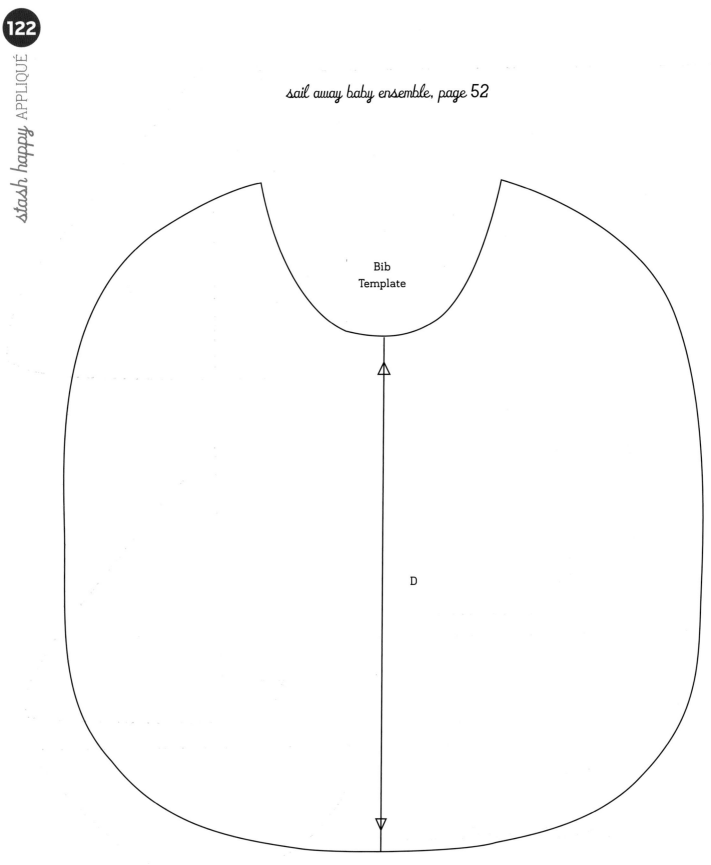

Bib
Template

D

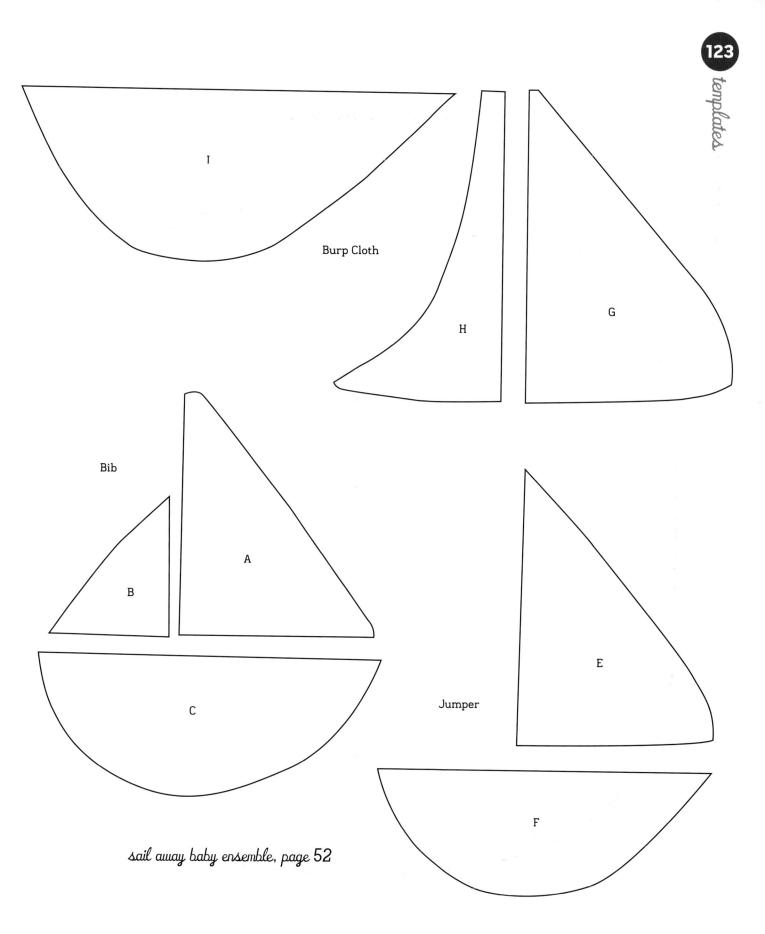

I

Burp Cloth

H

G

Bib

A

B

E

C

Jumper

F

sail away baby ensemble, page 52

stash happy APPLIQUÉ

woodsy gnome doll, page 70
(enlarge 150%)

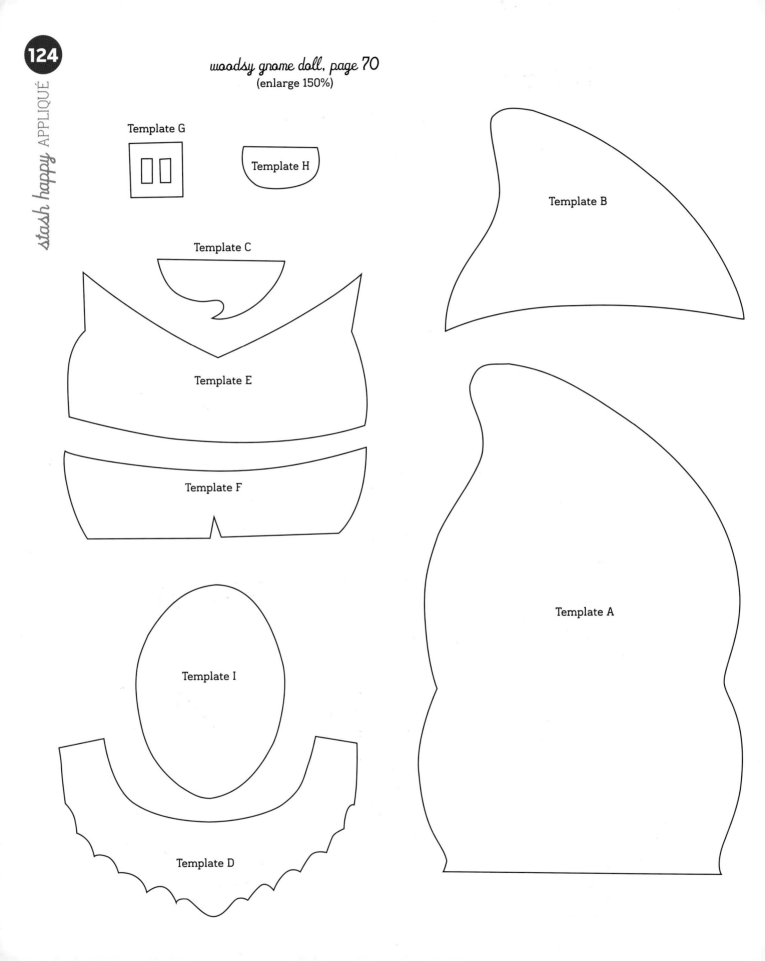

Template G

Template H

Template B

Template C

Template E

Template F

Template A

Template I

Template D

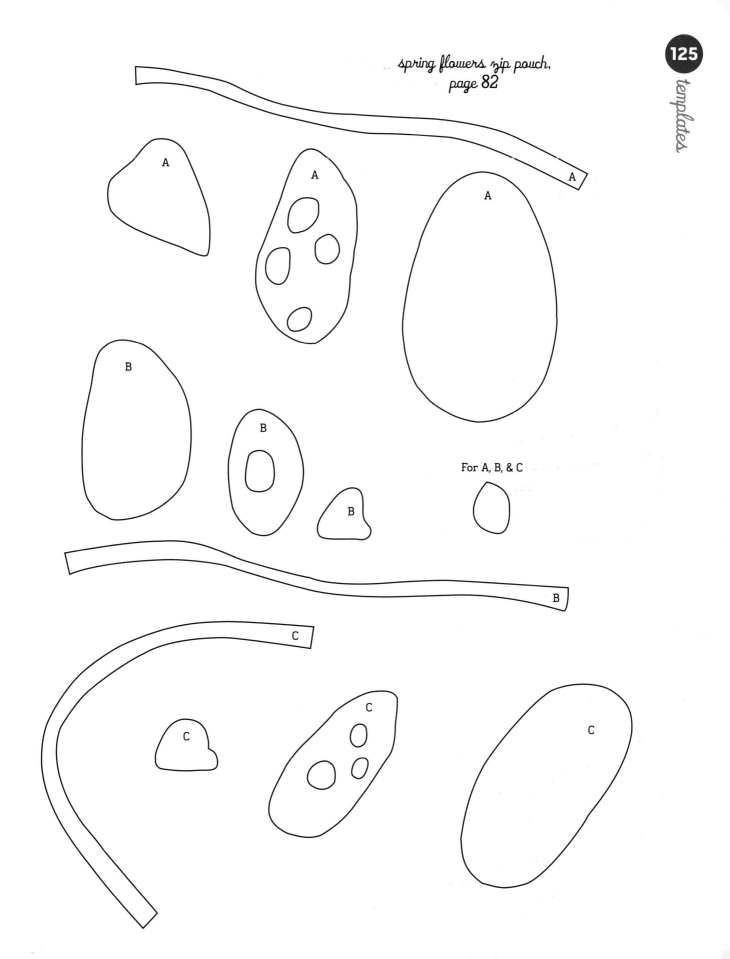

spring flowers zip pouch,
page 82

A

A

A

A

B

B

B

For A, B, & C

B

C

C

C

C

angel wings altered tee,
page 90
(enlarge 200%)

A

B

everyday mod skirt, page 86

A

B

C

fun & friendly furoshiki, page 74
(enlarge 200%)

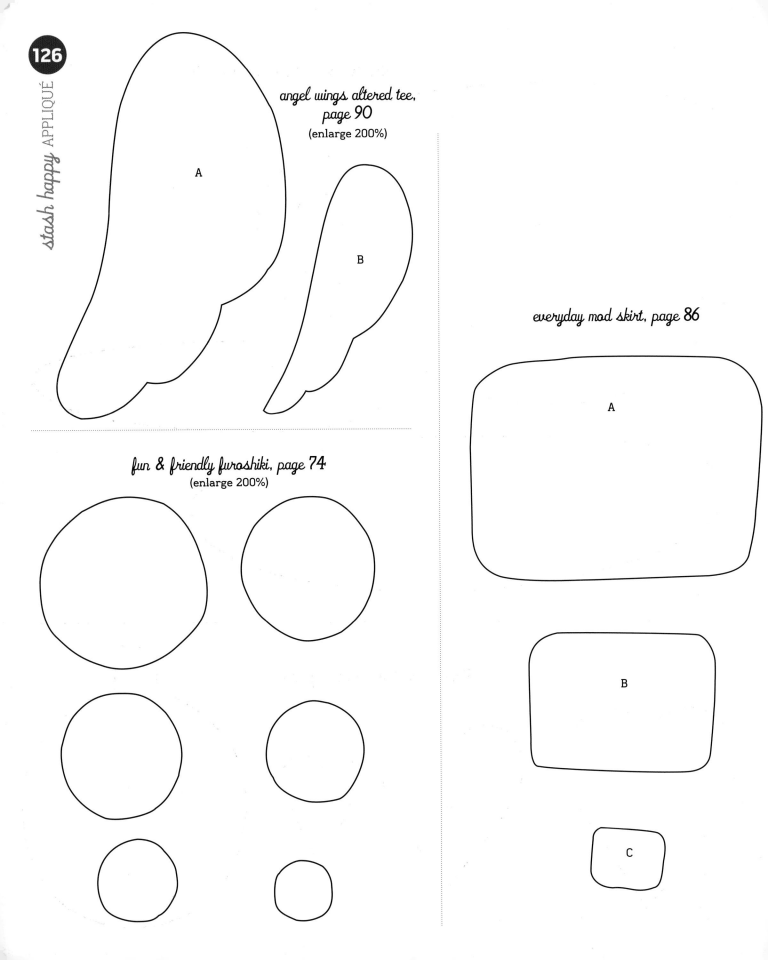

time for tea café curtains, page 34

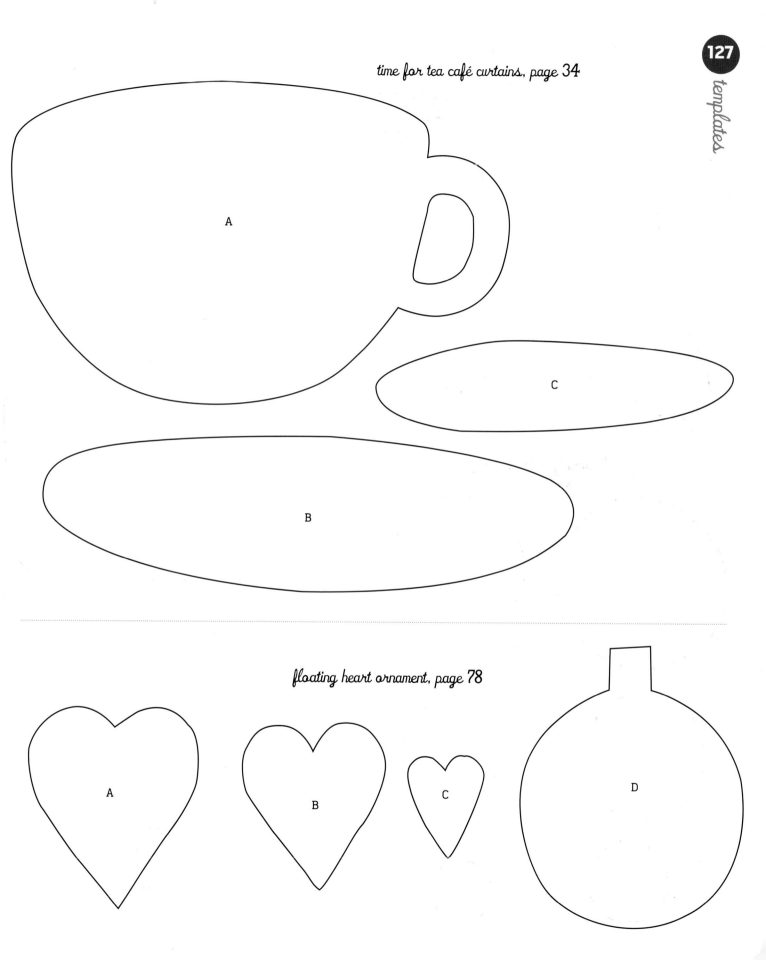

A

C

B

floating heart ornament, page 78

A

B

C

D

about the author

Cynthia Shaffer is author of *Stash Happy Patchwork*. She is a quilter and creative sewer whose love of fabric can be traced back to childhood. At the age of 6, she learned to sew and in no time was designing and sewing clothing for herself and others. After earning a degree in textiles from California State University, Long Beach, Cynthia worked for 10 years as the owner of a company that specialized in the design and manufacture of sportswear. Numerous books and magazines have featured Cynthia's work. She lives with her husband, Scott, sons, Corry and Cameron, and beloved dogs, Harper and Berklee, in Southern California. For more information, visit her online at www.cynthiashaffer.com.

acknowledgments

I'd like to thank the entire Lark Crafts family for believing in me and in this book. In particular, I am grateful to Thom O'Hearn and Amanda Carestio for their continued guidance and patience throughout the process. Also, many thanks to Moda Fabrics, Westminster Fibers, Windham Fabrics (Nature Inspired line by Tracie Lyn Huskamp), and Bari J. Ackerman for their donation of exquisite fabrics. Throughout my entire life, my mother and father encouraged me to do what I love, for which I am ever grateful. To my family—Scott, Corry, and Cameron—thank you for allowing me the space and time to focus on this project and for offering honest input and feedback that helped me work hard to get things just right. And finally to my friend and colleague, Jenny Doh—thank you for listening, imagining, and being with me to make it happen.

index

also in this series